ROAST IT

ROAST IT

PAVILION

This edition published in the United Kingdom
in 2014 by
Pavilion
1 Gower Street
London
WC1E 6HD

The Good Housekeeping website is
www.goodhousekeeping.co.uk

10 9 8 7 6 5 4 3 2

ISBN 978-1-909397-03-3

A catalogue record for this book is available from
the British Library.

Reproduction by Dot Gradations Ltd, UK
Printed and bound by
Times Offset (M) Sdn Bhd, Malaysia

This book can be ordered direct from the publisher.
Contact the marketing department, but try your
bookshop first.

www.pavilionbooks.com

NOTES

Both metric and imperial measures are given for
the recipes. Follow either set of measures, not a
mixture of both, as they are not interchangeable.

All spoon measures are level.
1 tsp = 5ml spoon; 1 tbsp = 15ml spoon.

Ovens and grills must be preheated to the specified
temperature.

Medium eggs should be used except where
otherwise specified. Free-range eggs are
recommended.

Note that some recipes contain raw or lightly
cooked eggs. The young, elderly, pregnant women
and anyone with an immune-deficiency disease
should avoid these because of the slight risk
of salmonella.

Contents

Perfect Poultry

Perfect Preparation

Chicken and other poultry such as turkey and duck are perfect for roasting. Roasting is also a simple way to cook young game birds.

Preparing the bird

Take the bird out of the fridge 45 minutes–1 hour before roasting to allow it to reach room temperature. Before stuffing a bird for roasting, clean it thoroughly. Put the bird in the sink and pull out and discard any loose fat with your fingers. Then dry the bird well using kitchen paper.

Trussing

It is not necessary to truss poultry before roasting it, but it gives the bird a neater shape for serving at the table.

1 Cut out the wishbone by pulling back the flap of skin at the neck end and locating the tip of the bone with a small sharp knife. Run the knife along the inside of the bone on both sides, then on the outside. Take care not to cut deep into the breast meat. Using poultry shears or sharp-pointed scissors, snip the tip of the bone from the breastbone and pull the bone away from the breast. Snip the two ends or pull them out by hand.

2 Pull off any loose fat from the neck or cavity. Put the wing tips under the breast and fold the neck flap on to the back of the bird. Thread a trussing needle and use it to secure the neck flap.

3 Push a metal skewer through both legs, at the joint between thigh and drumstick. Twist some string around both ends of the skewer and pull firmly to tighten.

4 Turn the bird over. Bring the string over the ends of the drumsticks, pull tight and tie to secure the legs.

Hygiene

- ❑ Raw poultry and meat contain harmful bacteria that can spread easily to anything they touch
- ❑ Always wash your hands, kitchen surfaces, chopping boards, knives and equipment before and after handling poultry or meat
- ❑ Don't let raw poultry or meat touch other foods
- ❑ Always cover raw poultry and meat and store in the bottom of the fridge, where they can't touch or drip on to other foods

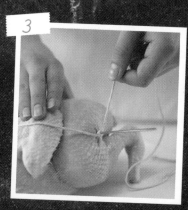

Poultry and Game
Perfect Roasting

Basting

Chicken, turkey and other poultry
needs to be basted regularly during
roasting to keep the flesh moist.
Use an oven glove to steady the
roasting tin and spoon the juices and
melted fat over the top of the bird.
Alternatively, use a bulb baster.

How to tell if poultry is cooked

- ❏ To check if chicken or turkey is
  cooked, pierce the thickest part
  of the meat – usually the thigh –
  with a skewer. The juices that run
  out should be golden and clear. If
  there are any traces of pink in the
  juice, put the bird back into the
  oven and cook for 10 minutes, then
  check again in the same way
- ❏ Duck and game birds are
  traditionally served with the meat
  slightly pink: if overcooked, the
  meat may be dry

Resting

Once the bird is cooked, allow it to
rest before carving.
Lift it out of the roasting tin, put it
on a plate and cover loosely with foil
and a clean teatowel. Resting allows
the juices to settle back into the meat,
leaving it moist and easier to carve.

Resting times

Grouse and small game birds	10 minutes
Chicken and duck	15 minutes
Turkey and goose	up to 1¼ hours

Poultry and game roasting times

Chicken

To calculate the roasting time for a chicken, weigh the oven-ready bird (including stuffing, if using) and allow 20 minutes per 450g (1lb), plus 20 minutes extra, in an oven preheated to 200°C (180°C fan oven) mark 6.

OVEN-READY WEIGHT	SERVES	COOKING TIME (APPROX.)
1.4-1.6 kg (3-3½lb)	4-6	1½ hours
1.8-2.3kg (4-5lb)	6-8	1 hour 50 minutes
2.5-2.7kg (5½-6lb)	8-10	2¼ hours

Turkey

Wrap loosely in a 'tent' of foil, then cook in an oven preheated to 190°C (170°C fan oven) mark 5. Allow 20 minutes per 450g (1lb), plus 20 minutes extra. Remove the foil about 1 hour before the end of cooking time to brown. Baste regularly.

OVEN-READY WEIGHT	SERVES	COOKING TIME (APPROX.)	
2.3-3.6kg (5-8lb)	4-8	15-18 hours	2-3 hours
3.6-5kg (8-11lb)	8-11	18-20 hours	3-3¼ hours
5-6.8kg (11-15lb)	11-15	20-24 hours	3¼-4 hours
6.8-9kg (15-20lb)	15-20	24-30 hours	4-5½ hours

Other poultry

Preheat the oven to 200°C (180°C fan oven) mark 6.

	SERVES	COOKING TIME (APPROX.)
Poussin	1-2	20 minutes per 450g (1lb)
Guinea fowl	1.4kg (3lb)	3-4	1½ hours
Duck	1.8-2.5kg (4-5½lb)	2-4	1½-2 hours
Goose, small	3.6-5.4kg (8-12lb)	4-7	20 minutes per 450g (1lb)
Goose, medium	5.4-6.3kg (12-14lb)	8-11	25 minutes per 450g (1lb)

Feathered game

Preheat the oven to 200°C (180°C fan oven) mark 6.

	SERVES	COOKING TIME (APPROX.)
Grouse	1-2	25-35 minutes
Partridge	2	20-25 minutes
Pheasant	2-4	45-60 minutes

Perfect Carving

Follow these tried and trusted steps for perfect carving results.

After resting, put the bird on a carving board.

1. Steady the bird with a carving fork. To cut breast meat, start at the neck end and cut slices about 5mm (¼in) thick. Use the carving knife and fork to lift them on to a warmed serving plate.

2. To cut off the legs, cut the skin between the thigh and breast.

3. Pull the leg down to expose the joint between the thigh bone and ribcage and cut through that joint.

4. Cut through the joint between the thigh and drumstick.

5. To carve meat from the leg (for turkeys and very large chickens), remove it from the carcass and joint the two parts of the leg, as above. Holding the drumstick by the thin end, stand it up on the carving board and carve slices roughly parallel with the bone. The thigh can be carved either flat on the board or upright.

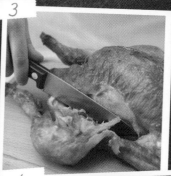

Poussins and small game birds

Poussins and other small birds such as grouse can serve one or two people. To serve two, you will need to split them. The easiest way to do this is with poultry shears and using a carving fork to steady the bird. Insert the shears between the legs and cut through the breastbone. As you do this, the bird will open out, exposing the backbone; cut through the backbone.

Storing leftovers

Don't forget the leftovers when the meal is finished – never leave poultry standing in a warm room. Cool quickly in a cold place, then cover and chill.

Roast Chicken with Stuffing and Gravy

Hands-on time: 30 minutes
Cooking time: about 1 hour 20 minutes, plus cooling and resting

1.4kg (3lb) chicken

2 garlic cloves

1 onion, cut into wedges

2 tsp sea salt

2 tsp freshly ground black pepper

4 sprigs each fresh parsley and tarragon

2 bay leaves

50g (2oz) butter, cut into cubes

For the stuffing

40g (1½oz) butter

1 small onion, chopped

1 garlic clove, crushed

75g (3oz) fresh white breadcrumbs

finely grated zest and juice of
   1 small lemon, halves put to one
   side for the chicken

2 tbsp each freshly chopped flat-leafed
   parsley and tarragon

1 medium egg yolk

salt and freshly ground black pepper

For the gravy

200ml (7fl oz) white wine

1 tbsp Dijon mustard

450ml (¾ pint) hot chicken stock
   (see page 155)

25g (1oz) butter, mixed with 25g (1oz)
   plain flour

1 Preheat the oven to 190°C (170°C fan oven) mark 5. To make the stuffing, melt the butter in a pan and fry the onion and garlic for 5–10 minutes until soft. Cool, then add the remaining ingredients, stirring in the egg yolk last. Season well with salt and ground black pepper.

2 Put the chicken on a board breast side up, then put the garlic, onion, reserved lemon halves and half the sea salt, pepper and herb sprigs into the cavity.

3 Lift the loose skin at the neck and fill the cavity with stuffing. Turn the bird

over on to its breast and pull the neck flap down and over the opening to cover the stuffing. Rest the wing tips across it and truss the chicken (see page 8). Weigh the stuffed bird to calculate the cooking time (see page 11).

4 Put the chicken on a rack in a roasting tin. Season, then add the remaining herbs and the bay leaves. Dot with the butter and roast, basting halfway through, until cooked and the juices run clear when the thickest part of the thigh is pierced with a skewer. If there are any traces of pink in the juice, put the bird back into the oven and cook for 10 minutes, then check again in the same way.

5 Transfer the chicken to a serving dish, cover loosely with foil and leave to rest while you make the gravy. Tilt the roasting tin and pour off all but about 3 tbsp fat. Put the tin on the hob over a high heat, add the wine and boil for 2 minutes. Add the mustard and hot stock and bring back to the boil. Gradually whisk in knobs of the butter mixture until smooth, then season with salt and ground black pepper. Carve the chicken and serve with the stuffing and gravy.

Serves 5

Summer Roast Chicken

Hands-on time: 25 minutes
Cooking time: about 1¾ hours, plus resting

100g (3½oz) feta, crumbled
50g (2oz) black olives, pitted and sliced
leaves from 2 fresh oregano sprigs, finely
    chopped
1 tbsp olive oil
1 medium chicken, about 1.6kg (3½lb)
1 lemon, halved
300g (11oz) cherry tomatoes
150g (5oz) couscous
a large handful of watercress
salt and freshly ground black pepper

1 Preheat the oven to 190°C (170°C
   fan oven) mark 5. Put half each of
   the feta, olives, oregano and oil into
   a small bowl with plenty of ground
   black pepper and stir together.
   Set aside.

2 Lift up the neck flap of the chicken
   and use your fingers to ease the skin
   gently away from the breast meat
   – work all the way down the sides
   of the breasts and towards the legs.
   Push the feta mixture between the
   skin and meat to cover the whole
   breast area. Pull the neck flap down
   and over and secure with a skewer
   or cocktail sticks. Put a lemon half in
   the cavity of the chicken.

3 Put the chicken into a medium-large
   roasting tin and drizzle the remaining
   oil over it. Season and roast for 1¼
   hours. Add the tomatoes to the tin and
   shake to coat in the oil, then return to
   the oven for a further 15 minutes or
   until the chicken is cooked through
   and the tomatoes have burst.

4 Carefully transfer the chicken to a
   board and put the tomatoes into a
   small serving bowl. Cover both with
   foil. Tilt the roasting tin and spoon
   off as much fat as possible, leaving
   behind the darker juices. Add the
   couscous to the roasting tin and stir
   to coat. Squeeze in the juice from the
   remaining lemon half, then pour in
   just enough boiling water to cover
   the couscous. Cover the tin well with
   clingfilm and leave to cook for 10
   minutes.

5 Fluff up the couscous with a fork and stir the watercress and remaining feta, olives and oregano through. Check the seasoning.

6 Allow the chicken to rest for at least 25 minutes before serving with the couscous and tomatoes.

SAVE EFFORT

Save on washing-up by making the couscous in the tin you've used to roast the chicken – it adds great flavour too.

Serves 4

Roast Curried Chicken

Hands-on time: 20 minutes
Cooking time: about 1½ hours, plus resting

5cm (2in) piece fresh root ginger

1 whole chicken (weight about 1.8kg/4lb)

1 lime, halved

40g (1½oz) butter, softened

2 tbsp mild curry paste

800g (1¾lb) new potatoes, halved if large

¾ tbsp plain flour

165ml can coconut milk

1 tsp brown sugar (optional)

salt and freshly ground black pepper

seasonal vegetables to serve

1   Preheat the oven to 190°C (170°C fan oven) mark 5. Roughly chop half the ginger (leave the skin on) and put into the cavity of the bird. Add the lime halves and tie the legs together. Put the chicken into a large sturdy roasting tin. Put the butter and half the curry paste into a small bowl and mix together. Spread over the top and sides of the bird. Cover with foil and roast for 40 minutes.

2   Carefully remove the foil and add the potatoes to the tin, turning them to coat in the buttery mixture. Put back into the oven and cook for a further 40 minutes or until the potatoes are tender and the chicken is cooked through. Lift the chicken out of the tin and put on a board. Cover loosely with foil and leave to rest. Put the potatoes into a serving dish and keep warm.

3   Tilt the roasting tin and spoon off and discard most of the fat. Put the tin on the hob over a medium heat and stir in the flour and remaining curry paste, then grate in the remaining ginger. Stirring constantly, add the coconut milk. Fill the empty coconut can with water and add to the pan. Bring to the boil, then reduce the heat and simmer, stirring, for 3–5 minutes until thickened. Check the seasoning and add the sugar, if needed. Serve the chicken, roasted potatoes and gravy with seasonal vegetables.

Serves 4

Clementine and Sage Turkey with Madeira Gravy

Hands-on time: 30 minutes
Cooking time: about 3 hours 40 minutes, plus resting

5.4kg (12lb) free-range turkey (put the giblets for stock to one side, if you like – see page 156. Spend as much as you can on your turkey – you'll notice the difference in the texture and taste)

3 firm clementines

20g pack fresh sage

100g (3½oz) butter, softened

500g (1lb 2oz) stuffing (see pages 28–30)

3 celery sticks

3 carrots, halved lengthways

salt and freshly ground black pepper

fried clementine halves and stuffing balls to garnish (optional)

For the Madeira Gravy

25g (1oz) plain flour

125ml (4fl oz) Madeira wine

300ml (½ pint) chicken stock (see page 155)

1 tbsp runny honey or redcurrant jelly, if needed

1 Remove the turkey from the fridge 1 hour before you stuff it to let it come up to room temperature.

2 Preheat the oven to 190°C (170°C fan oven) mark 5. Finely grate the zest from the clementines into a medium bowl. Halve the zest-free clementines and put to one side. Next, add 2 tbsp thinly sliced sage leaves (put the rest of the bunch to one side) to the bowl with the butter and plenty of seasoning and mix well.

3 Put the turkey, breast side up, on a board. Use tweezers to pluck any feathers from the skin. Loosen the skin at the neck end and use your fingers to ease the skin away from the breast meat, until 9cm (3½in) is free. Spread most of the butter between the skin and meat. Put the remaining flavoured butter to one side.

4   Spoon the cold stuffing into the neck cavity, pushing it down between the skin and breast meat and taking care not to overfill. Neaten the shape. Turn the turkey over on to its breast, pull the neck flap down and over the stuffing and secure the neck skin with a skewer or cocktail sticks. Weigh the turkey and calculate the cooking time, allowing 30–35 minutes per 1kg (2¼lb).

5   Make a platform in a large roasting tin with celery sticks and carrot halves and sit the turkey on top. Put the clementine halves and the remaining sage (stalks and all) into the turkey cavity, then rub the remaining flavoured butter over the breast of the bird. Tie the legs together with string, season the bird all over and cover loosely with foil.

6   Roast for the calculated time, removing the foil for the last 45 minutes of cooking, and basting at least three times during cooking. If the skin is browning too quickly, cover with foil again.

7   To check if the turkey is cooked, pierce the thickest part of the thigh with a skewer – the juices should run clear. If there are any traces of pink in the juice, put the bird back into the oven and cook for 10 minutes, then check again in the same way. Alternatively, use a meat thermometer – the temperature needs to read 78°C when inserted into the thickest part of the breast.

8   When the turkey is cooked, tip the bird so that the juices run into the tin, then transfer the turkey to a board (put the roasting tin for the Madeira Gravy to one side). Cover loosely with foil and clean teatowels to help keep the heat in. Leave to rest in a warm place for at least 30 minutes or up to 1¼ hours.

9   To make the gravy, tilt the roasting tin and spoon off most of the fat (leaving the vegetables in the tin). Put the tin on the hob over a medium heat and add the flour. Cook, stirring well with a wooden spoon, for 1 minute. Gradually add the Madeira, scraping up all the sticky bits from the bottom of the tin, then leave to bubble for a few minutes. Next, stir in the stock and leave to simmer, stirring occasionally, for 5 minutes. Check the seasoning and add the honey or redcurrant jelly if needed. Strain into a warmed gravy jug, or into a clean pan to reheat when needed.

10 To serve, unwrap the turkey and transfer to a warmed serving plate. Remove the skewer or cocktail sticks and garnish with the fried clementine halves and stuffing balls, if you like. Serve with the gravy.

SAVE TIME

Prepare the turkey to the end of step 5 up to one day ahead. Chill. Allow the stuffed turkey to come up to room temperature, then complete the recipe to serve.

Serves 8,
with leftovers

Lemon and Parsley Butter Roast Turkey

Hands-on time: 25 minutes
Cooking time: about 3½ hours, plus resting

5.4kg (12lb) free-range turkey (put the
giblets for stock to one side – see page
156. Spend as much as you can on
a good free-range or organic bird –
you'll notice the difference in both the
taste and the texture)

1 lemon, zested (put the lemon to
one side)

100g (3½oz) unsalted butter, softened

20g pack flat-leafed parsley, finely
chopped

500g (1lb 2oz) uncooked Herbed Bread
Stuffing (see page 26)

1 red onion, halved

5 fresh bay leaves (optional)

salt and freshly ground black pepper

fresh bay leaves and extra lemon halves
browned (cut-side down) in oil to
garnish (optional)

1 Remove the turkey from the fridge
   1 hour before you stuff it to let it come
   up to room temperature.

2 Preheat the oven to 190°C (170°C fan
   oven) mark 5. Put the lemon zest,
   butter, parsley and plenty of seasoning
   into a small bowl and mix well.

3 Put the turkey, breast side up, on a
   board. Use tweezers to pluck any
   feathers from the skin. Loosen the
   skin at the neck end and use your
   fingers to ease the skin gently away
   from breast meat, until about 9cm
   (3½in) is free. Spread the butter
   mixture between the skin and meat.

4 Spoon the cold stuffing into the neck
   cavity, pushing it down between the
   skin and breast meat and taking care
   not to overfill. Neaten the shape.
   Turn the turkey over on to its breast,
   pull the neck flap down and over
   the stuffing and secure the neck
   skin with a skewer or cocktail sticks.

Weigh the turkey and calculate the cooking time, allowing 30–35 minutes per 1kg (2¼lb).

5 Transfer the turkey to a large roasting tin. Cut the zested lemon in half and squeeze the juice over the bird. Put the juiced halves into the bird's cavity, together with the red onion halves and the bay leaves, if you like. Tie the legs together with string, season the bird all over and cover loosely with foil.

6 Roast for the calculated time, removing the foil for the last 30 minutes of cooking, and basting at least four times during cooking. If the skin is browning too quickly, cover with foil again.

7 To check if the turkey is cooked, pierce the thickest part of the thigh with a skewer – the juices should run clear. If there are any traces of pink in the juice, put the bird back into the oven and cook for 10 minutes, then check again in the same way. Alternatively, use a meat thermometer – the temperature needs to read 78°C when inserted into thickest part of the breast.

8 When the turkey is cooked, tip the bird so that the juices run into the tin, then transfer the turkey to a board (put the roasting tin for the gravy to one side, see page 158). Cover well with foil and clean teatowels to help keep the heat in, then leave to rest in a warm place for at least 30 minutes or up to 1¼ hours.

9 When ready to serve, put on a warmed plate or board, remove the string, skewer or cocktail sticks and garnish, if you like.

Serves 8, with leftovers

Herbed Bread Stuffing

Hands-on time: 20 minutes
Cooking time: about 45 minutes, plus cooling

75g (3oz) butter, plus extra to dot

1 onion, finely chopped

500g (1lb 2oz) fresh white breadcrumbs

1 tbsp dried mixed herbs

500ml (17 fl oz) vegetable stock (see
   page 154)

8 tbsp fresh mixed herbs, finely chopped,
   such as parsley, thyme, sage and mint,
   plus extra to garnish

2 celery sticks. finely chopped

2 Braeburn apples, skin on, cored and
   finely diced

1 tbsp ready toasted and chopped
   hazelnuts

4 smoked streaky bacon rashers
   (optional)

salt and freshly ground black pepper

1 Preheat the oven to 190°C (170°C fan
oven) mark 5. Heat the butter in a
large frying pan and gently cook the
onion for 10 minutes until softened.
Stir in the breadcrumbs and mix to
combine. Next add the dried herbs
and pour in the stock.

2 Mix in the fresh herbs, celery,
apples and hazelnuts, and check the
seasoning (don't stir too much or
the mixture might be too gluey). Put
500g (1lb 2oz) of the stuffing to one
side for the turkey.

3 Spoon the remaining stuffing into an
ovenproof serving dish (add some
extra stock if you prefer your stuffing
looser) and dot over some butter. Lay
over the bacon strips if you like.

4 Cook the stuffing in the serving dish
for 30 minutes until the bacon is crisp
and the stuffing is piping hot. Serve.

Serves 8

Perfect Stuffing

These stuffings are suitable for chicken, turkey or goose.
All can be made a day ahead and chilled overnight. Alternatively, –
with the exception of the wild rice stuffing – all can be frozen for up to one
month. Thaw overnight in the fridge before using to stuff the bird.

Orange, Sage and Thyme Stuffing

To serve eight, you will need:
2 tbsp olive oil, 1 large finely chopped onion, 2 crushed garlic cloves, 75g (3oz) fresh white breadcrumbs, 50g (2oz) toasted and chopped pinenuts, grated zest of 1 orange, plus 2–3 tbsp juice, 2 tbsp each finely chopped fresh thyme and sage, 1 medium egg yolk, beaten, salt and freshly ground black pepper.

1 Heat the oil and fry the onion and garlic gently for 5 minutes or until soft but not brown.
2 Put the remaining ingredients into a large bowl. Add the onion mixture, season and stir to bind, adding more orange juice if needed.

Rosemary and Lemon Stuffing

To serve four to six, you will need:
25g (1oz) butter, 1 finely chopped onion, 125g (4oz) fresh white breadcrumbs, 1 tbsp freshly chopped rosemary leaves, grated zest of 1 lemon, 1 medium egg, beaten, salt and freshly ground black pepper.

1 Melt the butter in a pan, then fry the onion over a low heat for 10–15 minutes until soft and golden. Tip into a bowl and leave to cool.
2 Add the breadcrumbs, rosemary leaves and lemon zest to the onion. Season well, then add the egg and stir to bind.

Bacon, Pecan and Wild Rice Stuffing

To serve eight, you will need:
900ml (1½ pints) hot chicken stock (see page 155), 1 bay leaf, 1 fresh thyme sprig, 225g (8oz) mixed long-grain and wild rice, 50g (2oz) unsalted butter, 225g (8oz) roughly chopped smoked streaky bacon, 2 finely chopped onions, 3 finely chopped celery sticks, ½ Savoy cabbage, chopped, 3 tbsp finely chopped fresh marjoram, 85g sachet sage and onion stuffing mix, 125g (4oz) chopped pecans.

1 Pour the stock into a pan, add the bay leaf and thyme and bring to the boil. Add the rice and cover the pan, then reduce the heat and cook according to the pack instructions. Drain if necessary, then tip into a large bowl and cool quickly, discarding the herbs.
2 Melt the butter in a large pan, add the bacon, onions and celery and cook over a medium heat for 10 minutes or until the onions are soft but not brown. Add the cabbage and marjoram and cook for 5 minutes, stirring regularly.

3 Add the cabbage mixture to the rice, together with the stuffing mix and pecans. Tip into a bowl and cool quickly.

Sausage, Cranberry and Apple Stuffing

To serve eight, you will need:
50g (2oz) butter, 1 finely chopped onion, 1 crushed garlic clove, 4 pork sausages (total weight about 275g/10oz), skinned and broken up, 75g (3oz) dried cranberries, 2 tbsp freshly chopped parsley, 1 red eating apple, salt and freshly ground black pepper.

1 Heat the butter in a pan, add the onion and cook over a medium heat for 5 minutes or until soft. Add the garlic and cook for 1 minute. Tip into a bowl and leave to cool. Add the sausages, cranberries and parsley, then cover and chill overnight, or freeze.
2 Core and chop the apple and add it to the stuffing. Season with salt and ground black pepper and stir well.

Pork, Chestnut and Orange Stuffing

To serve eight to ten, you will need:
50g (2oz) butter, 6 roughly chopped shallots, 4 roughly chopped celery sticks, 1 fresh rosemary sprig, snipped, 1 tbsp freshly chopped flat-leafed parsley, 175g (6oz) firm white bread, cut into rough dice, 2 cooking apples (total weight about 225g/8oz), peeled, cored and chopped, 125g (4oz) cooked, peeled (or vacuum-packed) chestnuts, roughly chopped, grated zest of 1 large orange, 450g (1lb) coarse pork sausage meat, salt and freshly ground black pepper.

1 Melt the butter in a large frying pan and fry the shallots, celery and rosemary gently for 10-12 minutes until the vegetables are soft and golden. Tip into a large bowl. Add the parsley, bread, apples, chestnuts and orange zest to the bowl. Season and mix well.
2 Divide the sausage meat into walnut-sized pieces. Fry, in batches, until golden and cooked through. Add to the bowl and stir to mix, then cool quickly.

Pork, Spinach and Apple Stuffing

To serve eight, you will need:
2 tbsp olive oil, 150g (5oz) finely chopped onion, 225g (8oz) fresh spinach, torn into pieces if the leaves are large, 2 sharp apples, such as Granny Smith, peeled, cored and cut into chunks, 400g (14oz) pork sausage meat, coarsely grated zest of 1 lemon, 1 tbsp freshly chopped thyme, 100g (3½oz) fresh white breadcrumbs, 2 large eggs, beaten, salt and freshly ground black pepper.

1 Heat the oil in a frying pan, add the onion and cook for 10 minutes or until soft. Increase the heat, add the spinach and cook until wilted.
2 Add the apples and cook, stirring, for 2-3 minutes, then leave to cool. When the mixture is cold, add the sausage meat, lemon zest, thyme, breadcrumbs and eggs, then season with salt and ground black and stir until evenly mixed.

Falafel Balls

These stuffing balls are delicious with turkey, but are also great with pitta bread and salad as a vegetarian meal.

To serve eight to ten, you will need: 275g (10oz) dried chickpeas, 1 small roughly chopped onion, a small handful of fresh coriander, 3 roughly chopped garlic cloves, juice of ½ lemon, 2 tsp ground cumin, ½ tsp bicarbonate of soda, olive oil to shallow-fry, salt and freshly ground black pepper.

1 Put the chickpeas into a pan and cover with plenty of cold water. Bring to the boil and boil for 2 minutes, then leave to soak for 2 hours. Drain.

2 Put the drained chickpeas into a food processor with the onion, coriander, garlic, lemon juice, cumin, bicarbonate of soda and ½ tsp salt and ground black pepper. Whiz until everything is finely ground and beginning to stick together. Take small handfuls of the mixture and squeeze in the palm of your hand to extract any excess moisture. Shape into walnut-sized balls.

3 Heat the oil in a frying pan over a medium-high heat and fry the falafel for 3-4 minutes until they turn a deep golden brown all over. Drain well on kitchen paper. Serve immediately, or chill for later use.

4 To use, put the falafel in a parcel of foil and reheat alongside the roast for 15-20 minutes.

Turkey Breast with Sausage, Cranberry and Apple Stuffing

🍴 **Hands-on time:** 25 minutes
Cooking time: about 1½ hours, plus resting

turkey breast joint (weight about
   1.4kg/3lb)

Sausage, Cranberry and Apple Stuffing,
   thawed (see page 29)

3 tbsp olive oil

1–2 tsp chicken seasoning

1 red eating apple

4–5 bay leaves

salt and freshly ground black pepper

For the gravy

1 tbsp plain flour

2 tbsp cranberry jelly

300ml (½ pint) dry cider

600ml (1 pint) hot chicken stock
   (see page 155)

1. Preheat the oven to 200°C (180°C fan oven) mark 6. Put three or four wooden skewers into a bowl of water to soak.

2. Put the turkey joint on a board, skin side down, and cut down the middle, along the length of the joint, to just over three-quarters of the way through. Season with salt and ground black pepper, spoon the stuffing inside, then push the joint back together. Secure with fine string and the soaked skewers. Weigh the joint, then calculate the cooking time, allowing 20 minutes per 450g (1lb), plus 20 minutes extra. For the specified 1.4kg (3lb) turkey, the cooking time will be about 1 hour 20 minutes.

3. Put the joint into a roasting tin, skin side up, drizzle with the oil and sprinkle with the chicken seasoning. Cover with foil and put into the oven.

4. Slice the apple into thin rounds. About 30 minutes before the end of the cooking time, remove the foil and push the apple slices and bay leaves under the string around the joint. Roast, uncovered, for the final

30 minutes or until cooked through – the juices should run clear when the thickest part of the meat is pierced with a skewer. If there are any traces of pink in the juice, put the joint back into the oven and cook for 10 minutes, then check again in the same way.

5   Transfer the turkey joint to a warmed plate, cover with foil and leave to rest for about 20 minutes.

6   To make the gravy, tilt the roasting tin and drain off all but about 1 tbsp fat. Add the flour and stir in. Put the tin on the hob over a medium heat and cook for 1 minute, scraping the pan to mix in all the juices. Stir in the cranberry jelly and cider, bring to the boil and bubble until the liquid has reduced by half. Add the hot stock and cook for about 5 minutes until the gravy has thickened slightly. Remove the skewers from the turkey, cut the meat into slices and serve with the gravy.

Serves 8

Poussins with Pancetta, Artichoke and Potato Salad

Hands-on time: 20 minutes, plus overnight marinating
Cooking time: 1 hour 40 minutes, plus resting

grated zest of 1 lemon

5 large fresh rosemary sprigs,
  leaves stripped

4 tbsp white wine vinegar

150ml (¼ pint) fruity white wine

4 garlic cloves, crushed

3 tbsp chopped fresh oregano or a pinch
  of dried oregano

290g jar marinated artichokes, drained,
  oil put to one side

3 poussins (each weighing about
  450g/1lb)

½ tsp cayenne pepper

450g (1lb) new potatoes, quartered

225g (8oz) pancetta or prosciutto or
  streaky bacon, roughly chopped

350g (12oz) peppery salad leaves, such
  as watercress, mustard leaf and rocket,
  washed and dried

salt and freshly ground black pepper

1 Put the lemon zest and rosemary
   leaves into a large bowl with the
   vinegar, wine, garlic, oregano and
   4 tbsp oil from the artichokes. Stir
   well. Using a fork, pierce the skin of
   the poussins in five or six places, then
   season well with ground black pepper
   and the cayenne pepper. Put the
   birds, breast side down, in the bowl
   and spoon the marinade over them.
   Cover and chill overnight.

2 Boil the potatoes in salted water for
   2 minutes. Drain. Preheat the oven to
   200°C (180°C fan oven) mark 6.

3 Lift the poussins from the marinade
   and place, breast side up, in a large
   roasting tin. Scatter the potatoes,
   pancetta, prosciutto or bacon and the
   artichokes around them and pour the
   marinade over. Cook for 1½ hours,
   basting occasionally, or until golden
   and cooked through.

4 Cut each poussin in half lengthways and keep them warm. Toss the salad leaves with about 5 tbsp of the warm cooking juices. Arrange the leaves on warmed plates, then top with the potatoes, pancetta, artichokes and poussins and serve.

SAVE MONEY

Use the oil drained from the artichokes to make a salad dressing.

Serves 6

Roast Duck with Orange Sauce

Hands-on time: 50 minutes
Cooking time: about 1¾ hours, plus resting

2 large oranges

2 large fresh thyme sprigs

2.3kg (5lb) duck, preferably with giblets

4 tbsp vegetable oil

2 shallots, chopped

1 tsp plain flour

600ml (1 pint) chicken stock (see page 155)

25g (1oz) caster sugar

2 tbsp red wine vinegar

100ml (3½fl oz) fresh orange juice

100ml (3½fl oz) fruity German white wine

2 tbsp orange liqueur, such as Grand Marnier (optional)

1 tbsp lemon juice

salt and freshly ground black pepper

fresh mint and Glazed Orange Wedges (see opposite) to garnish

mangetouts and broccoli to serve

1 Preheat the oven to 200°C (180°C fan oven) mark 6. Using a zester, remove strips of zest from the oranges. Put half the zest into a pan of cold water and bring to the boil, then drain and put to one side. Remove the pith from both oranges and cut the flesh into segments.

2 Put the thyme and unblanched orange zest inside the duck, then season. Rub the skin with 2 tbsp of the oil, sprinkle with salt and place, breast side up, on a rack over a roasting tin. Roast for 30 minutes, basting after 20 minutes, then turn the bird breast side down and roast for about 35 minutes, basting again after 20 minutes. Turn the bird breast side up and roast for a further 10 minutes or until just cooked and the juices run clear when the thickest part of the thigh is pierced with a skewer. If there are any traces of pink in the juice, put the bird back into the oven and cook for 10 minutes, then check again in the same way.

3 Meanwhile, cut the gizzard, heart and neck into pieces. Heat the remaining 2 tbsp oil in a heavy-based pan, add

the giblets and fry until dark brown. Add the shallots and flour and cook for 1 minute. Pour in the stock, bring to the boil and bubble until reduced by half; strain.

4 Put the sugar and vinegar into a heavy-based pan over a low heat until the sugar dissolves. Increase the heat and cook until it forms a dark caramel. Pour in the orange juice and stir. Cool, cover and put to one side.

5 Lift the duck off the rack and keep it warm. Tilt the roasting tin and skim all the fat off the juices to leave about 3 tbsp sediment. Stir the wine into the sediment, then put the tin over a medium heat on the hob, bring to the boil and bubble for 5 minutes or until syrupy. Add the stock mixture and orange mixture and bring back to the boil, then bubble until syrupy, skimming if necessary. To serve the sauce, add the blanched orange zest and segments. Add the orange liqueur, if you like, and lemon juice to taste.

6 Carve the duck and garnish with mint and glazed orange wedges. Serve with the orange sauce, mangetouts and broccoli.

Glazed Orange Wedges

To glaze oranges, quarter them or cut into wedges, dust with a little caster sugar and grill until caramelised.

Serves 4

Roast Guinea Fowl

Hands-on time: 20 minutes, plus marinating
Cooking time: 1¼ hours, plus resting

1 guinea fowl

2 lemons – grated zest and juice of one, one quartered lengthways

3 bay leaves

5 fresh thyme sprigs

1 tbsp black peppercorns, lightly crushed

25g (1oz) butter

150ml (¼ pint) hot chicken stock (see page 155)

roast potatoes and green beans to serve

For the gravy

2 tbsp redcurrant jelly

100ml (3½fl oz) dry white wine

salt and freshly ground black pepper

1 Put the guinea fowl into a bowl and add the lemon zest and juice, bay leaves, thyme and peppercorns. Cover and leave to marinate for 1 hour. Preheat the oven to 200°C (180°C fan oven) mark 6.

2 Put the bird into a roasting tin, breast side down, then put the lemon quarters and butter into the cavity, pour the hot stock over it and roast for 50 minutes.

3 Turn the guinea fowl breast side up and continue to roast for 20 minutes or until cooked and the juices run clear when the thigh is pierced with a skewer.

4 Transfer the guinea fowl to a board, cover loosely with foil and leave to rest for 10 minutes.

5 To make the gravy, put the roasting tin on the hob and scrape up the juices. Add the redcurrant jelly, wine and 50ml (2fl oz) water and bring to the boil, then reduce the heat and simmer for 3–5 minutes and season well. Carve the guinea fowl and serve with the gravy, roast potatoes and green beans.

Roast Grouse

Hands-on time: 10 minutes
Cooking time: 40 minutes, plus resting

2 oven-ready grouse

6 streaky bacon rashers

2 tbsp vegetable oil

2 tbsp roughly chopped fresh rosemary
   or thyme (optional)

salt and freshly ground black pepper

Parsnip and Potato Crisps (see below)
   or hand-cooked salted crisps and
   watercress to serve

Parsnip and Potato Crisps

Using a vegetable peeler, cut thin strips
off each vegetable. Heat a pan half full of
sunflower oil until a small cube of bread
browns in 20 seconds. Fry the strips,
a few at a time, until golden. Drain on
kitchen paper and serve immediately.

1 Preheat the oven to 200°C (180°C fan
   oven) mark 6. Put the grouse into a
   large roasting tin, with enough space
   between them so that they can brown
   evenly. Cover the breast of each with
   rashers of bacon, drizzle with 1 tbsp
   of the oil, then season with salt and
   ground black pepper. Sprinkle with
   herbs, if you like.

2 Roast for about 40 minutes until the
   juices run clear when the thigh is
   pierced with a skewer.

3 Transfer the grouse to a board, cover
   loosely with foil and leave to rest for
   10 minutes.

4 Serve with the Parsnip and Potato
   crisps or ready-made hand-cooked
   crisps, plus watercress to contrast
   with the richness of the meat.

Serves 4

Perfect Pork

Honey Pork with Roast Potatoes and Apples

Hands-on time: 20 minutes
Cooking time: 1¾ hours, plus resting

1kg (2¼lb) loin of pork, with crackling
    and four bones, at room temperature

4 tbsp olive oil

25g (1oz) butter

700g (1½lb) Charlotte potatoes,
    scrubbed and halved

1 large onion, cut into eight wedges

2 Cox's apples

1 tbsp runny honey mixed with 1 tbsp
    wholegrain mustard

12 fresh sage leaves

175ml (6fl oz) dry cider

salt and freshly ground black pepper

1   Preheat the oven to 240°C (220°C fan
    oven) mark 9. Put the pork on a board
    and use a paring knife to score the
    skin into thin strips, cutting about
    halfway into the fat underneath. Rub
    1 tsp salt and 2 tbsp of the oil over
    the skin and season well with ground
    black pepper. Put the meat on a rack,
    skin side up, over a large roasting
    tin (or just put the pork in the tin).
    Roast for 25 minutes. Reduce the
    oven temperature to 190°C (170°C fan
    oven) mark 5 and continue to roast
    for 15 minutes.

2   Add the remaining oil and the
    butter to the roasting tin. Scatter the
    potatoes and onion around the meat,
    season with salt and ground black
    and continue to roast for 45 minutes.

3   Meanwhile, core the apples and cut
    each into six wedges. Take the roasting
    tin out of the oven and brush the meat
    with the honey and mustard mixture.
    Add the apples and sage leaves to the
    tin and roast for a further 15 minutes or
    until the pork is cooked.

4   Remove the pork from the tin and
    wrap completely with foil, then leave
    to rest for 10 minutes. Turn down the
    oven to 150°C (130°C fan oven) mark
    2. Put the potatoes, onions and apples
    into a warmed serving dish and put

back in the oven to keep warm.

5 Tilt the roasting tin and pour off as much of the fat as you can, leaving just the dark brown juices. Put the roasting tin on the hob over a medium heat, add the cider and stir well to make a thin gravy. Season.

6 Cut the meat away from the bone. Cut between each bone. Pull the crackling away from the meat and cut into strips. Carve the joint, giving each person some crackling and a bone to chew. Serve with the gravy and potatoes, onion and apples.

Serves 4

45

Perfect Loin of Pork

Loin of pork fillet can be cooked on or off the bone. Boned loin of pork may be rolled with or without stuffing, and with or without the skin – which makes the crispy crackling. You can buy boned, rolled and tied pork loin, but if you want to stuff it you will need to tie it yourself.

1 Trim away excess fat and sinews. Shape the stuffing into a thin sheet or cylinder. Lay the loin with the fat side down on the chopping board and put the stuffing on the line where the eye of loin meets the flap meat. Fold the flap of meat over the eye and secure with skewers.

2 Tie the loin with string every 5cm (2in) and remove the skewers.

Perfect crackling
- ❑ If possible, ask the butcher to score the skin for you
- ❑ The pork skin needs to be dry. Remove the shop's wrapping and pat the skin dry with kitchen paper
- ❑ Leave the joint uncovered in the fridge overnight to dry out the skin
- ❑ Use a craft knife or your sharpest knife to score the skin, cutting about halfway into the fat underneath
- ❑ Rub the scored skin with a little olive oil and salt

1

Pork roasting times

Preheat the oven to 180°C (160°C fan oven) mark 4.

Note Many cooks give pork an initial blast of heat – 220°C (200°C fan oven) mark 7 or even higher – for 15–20 minutes before reducing the temperature. If you do this, watch it carefully near the end of its cooking time.

OFF THE BONE	COOKING TIME PER 450G (1LB)
Well done	25–30 minutes
ON THE BONE	**COOKING TIME PER 450G (1LB)**
Well done	30–35 minutes

Use the times above as a guideline, but remember that cooking times will vary depending on how the meat has been aged and stored, the shape and thickness of the joint and personal taste. Ovens vary as well. If a recipe gives a different oven temperature, follow the recipe for timing.

How to tell if pork is cooked

To check if pork is cooked, pierce the thickest part of the meat with a skewer. The juices that run out should be golden and clear. If there are any traces of pink in the juice, put back into the oven and cook for 10–15 minutes, then check again in the same way.

Resting

When the pork is cooked, cover loosely with foil and leave to rest for 30 minutes before carving. Larger joints can rest for up to 45 minutes without getting cold.

Carving pork with crackling

1 It is much easier to slice pork if you first remove the crackling. Remove any string and position the carving knife just under the skin on the topmost side of the joint. Work the knife under the crackling, taking care not to cut into the meat, until you can pull it off with your fingers.

2 Slice the meat, then snap the crackling into servings.

Crisp Roast Pork with Apple Sauce

Hands-on time: 30 minutes, plus standing
Cooking time: about 2¼ hours, plus resting

1.6kg (3½lb) boned rolled loin of pork

olive oil

1kg (2¼lb) cooking apples, cored and roughly chopped

1–2 tbsp granulated sugar

1 tbsp plain flour

600ml (1 pint) chicken stock (see page 155) or dry cider

salt and freshly ground black pepper

new potatoes and green vegetables to serve

1 Score the pork skin, sprinkle generously with salt and leave at room temperature for 1–2 hours.

2 Preheat the oven to 220°C (200°C fan oven) mark 7. Wipe the salt off the skin, rub with oil and sprinkle again with salt. Put half the apples into a small roasting tin, sit the pork on top and roast for 30 minutes. Reduce the oven temperature to 190°C (170°C fan oven) mark 5 and roast for a further 1½ hours or until cooked.

3 Meanwhile, put the remaining apples into a pan with the sugar and 2 tbsp water, cover with a tight-fitting lid and cook until just soft. Put to one side.

4 Transfer the pork to a serving dish, cover loosely with foil and leave to rest while you make the gravy. Skim off most of the fat in the roasting tin, leaving about 1 tbsp and the apples. Put the tin on the hob over a medium heat. Stir in the flour until smooth, then stir in the stock or cider and bring to the boil. Bubble gently for 2–3 minutes, skimming if necessary. Strain the sauce through a sieve into a jug, pushing through as much of the apple as possible. Slice the pork and serve with the sauce, new potatoes and green vegetables.

Serves 6

Fennel Roast Pork

Hands-on time: 25 minutes
Cooking time: about 1½ hours, plus resting

4 fresh rosemary sprigs

6 large garlic cloves

3 tsp fennel seeds

1.6kg (3½lb) loin of pork, boned, at room
   temperature

300ml (½ pint) dry white wine

salt and freshly ground black pepper

mashed potatoes and curly kale to serve

1 Preheat the oven to 220°C (200°C
   fan oven) mark 7. Put two rosemary
   sprigs to one side, then strip the
   leaves off the remainder. Put the
   garlic, rosemary leaves, fennel seeds,
   1 tsp salt and 1 tsp ground black
   pepper into a food processor and mix
   to a smooth paste.

2 Score the fat side of the pork with a
   sharp knife, then rub the flesh side
   with the garlic and rosemary paste.

Rub salt over the fat side. Roll up
the loin, then tie along its length at
2.5cm (1in) intervals with fine string.
Weigh the meat and calculate the
cooking time, allowing 25 minutes
per 450g (1lb).

3 Heat a roasting tin on the hob and
   brown the pork all over, then add
   the wine and remaining rosemary
   sprigs. Put into the oven and roast
   for 20 minutes, then reduce the
   oven temperature to 200°C (180°C
   fan oven) mark 6 and roast for the
   remaining calculated time.

4 Transfer the meat to a board, cover
   loosely with foil and leave to rest for
   15 minutes. Slice the pork and serve
   with the pan juices poured over, with
   mashed potatoes and curly kale.

Serves 6

Cider Roast Pork

Hands-on time: 10 minutes, plus marinating
Cooking time: about 1½ hours, plus resting

1.1kg (2½lb) boned rolled loin of pork, fat removed

1 tbsp olive oil

2 red onions, quartered

2 apples, cored and quartered

a few fresh thyme sprigs, chopped

440ml can dry cider

salt and freshly ground black pepper

cabbage to serve

1   Put the pork into a bowl, then add the oil, onions, apples and thyme. Pour in the cider, cover and marinate in the fridge for 4 hours or overnight.

2   Take the pork out of the fridge 1 hour before roasting to allow it to come up to room temperature. Preheat the oven to 200°C (180°C fan oven) mark 6. Put the pork into a roasting tin with the marinade ingredients and season. Roast for about 1½ hours until the pork is cooked. Remove the pork from the roasting tin and leave to rest.

3   To make the cider gravy, drain the roasting juices into a pan, bring to the boil and bubble for 5 minutes until reduced. Slice the pork and serve with the gravy and cabbage.

Pork and Sage Parcel

Hands-on time: 15 minutes
Cooking time: about 30 minutes, plus resting

375g pack ready-rolled puff pastry
1 medium egg, beaten
75g (3oz) pancetta slices
2 × 400g (14oz) pork fillets, membrane
   removed
1 tbsp freshly chopped sage
freshly ground black pepper
Roast Baby Potatoes (see page 146),
   Spiced Red Cabbage (see page 148)
   and Apple Sauce (see page 164)
   to serve

1 Preheat the oven to 220°C (200°C fan
   oven) mark 7. Unroll the puff pastry
   and cut out an 11.5 × 28cm (4½ × 11in)
   rectangle. Transfer to a baking tray
   and brush with some of the egg.

2 Arrange the pancetta slices side by
   side on a board, overlapping them
   a little. Lay one of the pork fillets
   horizontally across the middle of the
   pancetta slices. Press the sage on top
   of the pork, then season well with
   ground black pepper. Top with the
   second pork fillet.

3 Fold the pancetta around the pork
   and put the wrapped fillet, seam
   side down, on top of the pastry base.
   Cut 5mm (¼in) wide strips from the
   remaining pastry, each long enough
   to cover the fillet. Arrange the pastry
   strips in a crisscross pattern over the
   pork, pressing the ends of the strips to
   the base to help them stick. Brush the
   strips with the rest of the beaten egg.

4 Cook the pork parcel in the oven for
   25–30 minutes until the pastry is dark
   golden. Transfer to a board, cover with
   foil and leave to rest for 10 minutes.

5 Serve in slices with Roast Baby
   Potatoes, Spiced Red Cabbage and
   some Apple Sauce.

Prepare the parcel to the end of step 3 up to 3 hours ahead. Chill. Complete step 4 to serve, cooking the parcel for 30–35 minutes.

A stack of pork fillets, also known as tenderloins, make an inexpensive, quick and meltingly tender roast.

Serves 6

Stuffed Rack of Pork with Cider Gravy

Hands-on time: 30 minutes
Cooking time: about 2½ hours, plus resting

6 pork and apple sausages (total weight
about 400g/14oz)

a large handful of fresh parsley,
finely chopped

finely grated zest of 1 lemon

2 tbsp wholegrain mustard

2kg (4½lb) pork rack at room
temperature

2 onions, sliced in thick rings

salt and freshly ground black pepper

For the gravy

2 tbsp plain flour

200ml (7fl oz) cider

500ml (17fl oz) chicken stock
(see page 155)

1 tbsp runny honey or redcurrant jelly

½ tbsp wholegrain mustard

1. Preheat the oven to 220°C (200°C fan oven) mark 7. Peel off and discard the sausage skins. Put the meat into a medium bowl and mix in the parsley, lemon zest, mustard and some ground black pepper (the sausages should provide enough salt).

2. Make a 'flap' along the length of the joint by partially cutting the skin and fat away from the meat. Press the sausage mixture into this space, then tie the skin flap in place with string around the joint, along its length. Weigh the joint and calculate the cooking time, allowing 25 minutes per 450g (1lb).

3. Keeping the onion rings intact, arrange in the bottom of a roasting tin just large enough to hold the meat. Rest the pork on top, skin side up.

4. Season the skin with salt and roast for the calculated time, reducing the oven temperature to 180°C (160°C fan oven) mark 4 after the first 40 minutes. Continue cooking for the calculated time or until the juices run clear when the meat is pierced deeply with a knife. If using a meat thermometer, the temperature should hit 70°C in the thickest part of the joint.

5. Transfer the pork to a board and cover loosely with foil. Leave to rest in a warm place for at least 30 minutes while you make the gravy.

6. Tilt the roasting tin and spoon off all but 1 tbsp of the fat. Put the tin on the hob over a medium heat, sprinkle in the flour and stir, scraping up all the meaty bits stuck to the bottom. Take off the heat and gradually mix in the cider. Put back on to the heat and bubble for 2 minutes, stirring often. Add the stock and bring to the boil, then reduce the heat and simmer for 15 minutes or until the gravy reaches the desired consistency.

7. Strain the gravy into a warmed gravy boat, or into a clean pan (to reheat later) and stir in the honey or jelly, the mustard and any juices that have leaked from the pork. Check the seasoning. Put to one side to reheat or serve immediately with the meat.

Prepare the pork to the end of step 3 up to one day ahead. Cover and chill. To cook, allow to come up to room temperature, then dry the skin with kitchen paper before roasting and complete steps 4, 5, 6 and 7 to finish the recipe.

Rest the joint for up to 1 hour. If the crackling softens under the foil, pop it under a hot grill for a few minutes to crisp it up.

If there's no time to make a gravy after the pork has cooked, there's still a stress-free way to do it. Transfer the joint to a clean roasting tin 30 minutes before the end of cooking (continue cooking in a new tin). There will be enough juices in the original pan to make cider gravy while the joint is cooking.

An easy way to carve this joint is to first remove the bones in one go by slicing down just above them. Then simply slice the meat.

Serves 8-10

Perfect Roast Pork Belly

🍴 **Hands-on time:** 15 minutes, plus drying
Cooking time: about 3½ hours, plus resting

1.5kg (3lb 2oz) piece pork belly

salt

1 Using a small sharp knife, score lines into the pork skin (cutting into the fat) about 1cm (½in) apart, but not so deep that you cut into the meat. Pat the pork completely dry, then leave uncovered at room temperature to air dry for about 45 minutes.

2 Preheat the oven to 220°C (200°C fan) mark 7. Rub lots of salt over the pork skin. Rest a wire rack above a deep roasting tin and put the pork, skin side up, on the rack. Roast for 30 minutes, then reduce the oven temperature to 170°C (150°C fan oven) mark 3 and cook for 3 hours more – by this stage the crackling should be crisp and golden (if not, don't panic – see Save Effort right).

3 Transfer the pork to a board and use a sharp knife to slice off the crackling in one piece (about the outer 2cm/¾in). Cover the pork meat loosely with foil and leave to rest for 30–40 minutes.

4 Cut the crackling into six long strips, then cut the pork belly into six neat squares. Serve each square topped with a strip of crackling.

SAVE EFFORT

If your crackling isn't as crispy as you'd like, you can still rescue it. Remove the crackling and preheat the grill to medium-high. Put the whole piece of crackling on a baking tray and grill until crisp and puffed (watch carefully to avoid scorching, turning the tray to avoid any hot spots). Complete the recipe to serve.

Serves 6

Perfect Ham

Hams come in different sizes and cures; some are sold cooked, others are uncooked. Some need to be soaked, so buy your ham from a butcher and ask his advice on preparation and cooking.

Preparing and cooking ham

1 If the ham needs to be soaked, place it in a large container that will hold it comfortably with plenty of space for water. Pour cold water over it to cover and weigh down the ham if necessary. Leave to soak overnight, then drain well.

2 Put the ham into a large flameproof casserole, cover with cold water. Add a few sprigs of parsley, a few peppercorns, a bay leaf and a chopped onion to the water, if you like. Bring to just below boiling point – do not let the water boil or the meat will be tough. Skim off any surface scum. Simmer gently for 25 minutes per 450g (1lb), checking occasionally to make sure it is completely covered with water.

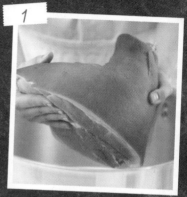

1

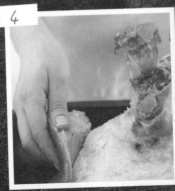

4

5

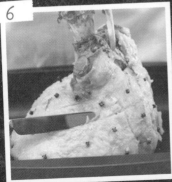

6

3 Leave to cool in the water. Transfer the ham to a roasting tin. (Put the stock for soup to one side.)

4 Preheat the oven to 200°C (180°C fan oven) mark 6. Remove the rind and neatly trim the fat so that there is a 5mm–1cm (¼–½in) layer left on the meat.

5 Score the fat with parallel lines about 5cm (2in) apart, then score on the diagonal to make diamond shapes. Press a clove into the centre of each diamond.

6 Spread prepared English mustard thinly and evenly over the ham – or glaze as the recipe suggests. Sprinkle with soft brown sugar to make a light but even coating. Bake the ham for about 30 minutes until golden brown.

Quick Roast Ham

Pressure Cooker Recipe

🍴 **Hands-on time:** 20 minutes
Cooking time: about 40 minutes

1kg (2¼lb) unsmoked boneless gammon joint

6 whole allspice berries

2–3 sprigs each fresh thyme and parsley

6 black peppercorns

225g (8oz) baby carrots

225g (8oz) baby leeks

225g (8oz) baby parsnips, halved

225g (8oz) shallots, halved if large

2 small green cabbages (total weight about 450g/1lb), quartered

3 tbsp wholegrain mustard

3 tbsp runny honey

3 tbsp olive oil

salt and freshly ground black pepper

1 Put the gammon into a pressure cooker. Pour in enough water to half-fill the pan, then add the allspice, thyme, parsley and peppercorns. Cover, put to the highest setting and bring up to pressure. Following the manufacturer's instructions, cook for 25 minutes. If your pressure cooker doesn't have a steam quick-release system, run the cold tap in the sink and hold the pan underneath it to reduce the pressure quickly. Lift out the gammon, then cover and put to one side.

2 Bring the stock back to the boil. Add the carrots, leeks, parsnips, shallots and cabbages and blanch for 2 minutes. Drain well, discarding the stock.

3 Preheat the oven to 240°C (220°C fan oven) mark 9. Put the ham into a roasting tin along with the blanched vegetables. Mix the mustard with the honey and 1 tbsp of the oil and drizzle over the ham. Pour the rest of the oil over the vegetables and season. Roast for 10–15 minutes until golden. Slice the ham and serve hot with the vegetables.

SAVE MONEY

Instead of discarding the stock at step 2, chill or freeze it; use to make soup.

Serves 4

Maple, Ginger and Soy Roast Gammon

Hands-on time: 10 minutes, plus soaking (optional)
Cooking time: about 2¼ hours

2 × 2.5kg (5½lb) smoked boneless
   gammon joints

8 tbsp vegetable oil

7.5cm (3in) piece fresh root ginger,
   peeled and grated

8 tbsp maple syrup

6 tbsp dark soy sauce

12 star anise (optional)

1 If the gammon is salty (check with
   your butcher), soak it in cold water
   overnight. Alternatively, bring to
   the boil in a large pan of water, then
   reduce the heat and simmer for 10
   minutes, then drain.

2 Preheat the oven to 200°C (180°C fan
   oven) mark 6. Put the joints into a
   roasting tin and pour 4 tbsp of the oil
   over them. Cover with foil and roast
   for 1 hour 50 minutes, or 20 minutes
   per 450g (1lb).

3 Mix the ginger, maple syrup, soy
   sauce and the remaining oil in a bowl.

4 Take the gammon out of the oven,
   remove the foil and leave to cool a
   little, then carefully peel away the
   skin and discard. Score the fat in a
   crisscross pattern, stud with the star
   anise, if you like, then pour the ginger
   sauce over the gammon. Continue to
   roast for another 20 minutes or until
   the glaze is golden brown. Slice and
   serve one joint warm. Cool the other,
   wrap in foil and chill until needed.

SAVE EFFORT

Home-cooked ham is great hot or
cold, but cooking a large joint is
often impractical. Roasting two
medium joints at the same time
means you can serve a hot joint and
have plenty left to eat cold.

Serves 18

Perfect Lamb

Roast Lamb and Boulangère Potatoes

Hands-on time: 25 minutes
Cooking time: about 1½ hours, plus resting

2kg (4½lb) Maris Piper potatoes, thinly
  sliced into rounds – a mandolin is
  ideal for this

1 large onion, thinly sliced

10 thyme sprigs

400ml (14fl oz) hot chicken stock (see
  page 155)

2 camomile teabags

2 tsp sunflower oil

1.6kg (3½lb) lamb shoulder at room
  temperature

salt and freshly ground black pepper

mint sauce or redcurrant jelly and
  seasonal vegetables to serve

1   Preheat the oven to 200°C (180°C fan
    oven) mark 6. Layer the potato slices,
    onion and half the thyme in a 2.5
    litre (4¼ pint) heatproof serving dish,
    seasoning as you go. Pour the hot
    stock over. Put a large wire rack over
    the dish.

2   Empty the contents of the camomile
    teabags into a small bowl (discard
    the bags). Stir in the leaves from the
    remaining thyme, some seasoning
    and the oil. Rub the camomile
    mixture over the lamb. Sit the lamb
    on the wire rack on top of the dish.
    Cover everything with foil.

3   Carefully transfer the dish to the
    oven and roast for 1 hour. Uncover
    and cook for 30 minutes more (the
    lamb should be cooked to medium)
    or until the lamb is cooked to your
    liking and the potatoes are tender
    and golden.

4   Transfer the lamb to a board,
    cover with foil and leave to rest
    for 20 minutes; keep the potatoes
    warm in the oven. Serve the lamb
    and potatoes with mint sauce
    or redcurrant jelly and seasonal
    vegetables.

Slow-roast Lamb Shoulder

Hands-on time: 20 minutes
Cooking time: about 4 hours 10 minutes, plus resting

4 canned anchovy fillets, chopped

finely grated zest of 1 lemon

3 fresh rosemary sprigs, leaves picked
and chopped

2 tbsp olive oil

2kg (4½lb) lamb shoulder (on the bone)
at room temperature

1 large onion, unpeeled and cut into
thick rings

5 unpeeled garlic cloves

salt and freshly ground black pepper

For the gravy

2 tbsp cornflour

100ml (3½fl oz) white wine

a small handful of fresh mint

1   Preheat the oven to 220°C (200°C
    fan) mark 7. Put the anchovy fillets,
    lemon zest, rosemary, oil and plenty of
    seasoning into a small bowl and mix
    well. Next, lay the lamb shoulder on a
    board and slash the fatty side well with
    a sharp knife. Rub the marinade all over
    the lamb.

2   Put the onions and garlic into a roasting
    tin just large enough to hold the lamb.
    Lay the lamb on top, slashed side up,
    and cover the tin with foil. Reduce the
    oven temperature to 170°C (150°C) mark
    3. Slow-roast for 4 hours, removing the
    foil for the last 45 minutes to allow the
    lamb to brown. The lamb is ready when
    you can shred the meat off the bone
    with two forks.

3   Transfer the lamb to a board and cover
    again with foil while you make the
    gravy – the lamb can rest happily for up
    to 45 minutes.

4   Tilt the roasting tin and pour off most
    of the fat (leaving the onions and garlic
    in place). Whisk in the cornflour, then
    the wine and mint (stalks and all). Bring
    to the boil, whisking frequently (and
    squishing the vegetables) until the
    gravy thickens. Add about 200ml
    (7fl oz) water and simmer until the
    gravy reaches the desired consistency.
    Strain, then taste and check the
    seasoning. Serve with the lamb.

Serves 8

Herbed Crown Roast of Lamb

Hands-on time: 10 minutes
Cooking time: about 35 minutes, plus resting

16-bone crown roast of lamb (weight about 800g/1lb 12oz), at room temperature

25ml (1fl oz) olive oil

5 fresh thyme sprigs, leaves removed

20g (¾oz) fresh flat-leafed parsley

1 large garlic clove, roughly chopped

1 tbsp Dijon mustard

salt and freshly ground black pepper

1 Preheat the oven to 200°C (180°C fan oven) mark 6. Put the lamb crown ring on a baking tray. Put the remaining ingredients and plenty of salt and ground black pepper into a blender (or pestle and mortar) and whiz (or bash together) until well combined.

2 Rub the herb mixture over the lamb, then roast for 30–35 minutes for pink meat (roast for longer if you like meat more cooked). Take the tray out of the oven and transfer the lamb to a board. Cover loosely with a few layers of foil and leave to rest for 20–30 minutes.

3 To serve, slice the crown into 16 cutlets (cutting between the bones).

SAVE TIME

Rub the herb mixture over the lamb up to 3 hours ahead, then chill. Take the lamb out of the fridge 40 minutes before roasting to allow it to come up to room temperature, then complete the recipe.

SAVE EFFORT

Remember to order a crown roast in advance and ask your butcher to prepare it for you.

Perfect Roast Lamb

From tender juicy noisettes of lamb to boned or butterflied leg of lamb for roasting, or rack of lamb tied in the French style or as an elegant guard of honour, lamb is wonderfully versatile.

Preheat the oven to 220°C (200°C fan oven) mark 7. Weigh the joint to calculate the roasting time. Brown the lamb in the hot oven for 20 minutes, then reduce the oven temperature to 190°C (170°C fan oven) mark 5 and roast for the calculated time.

	COOKING TIME PER 450G (1LB)
Medium	15–20 minutes
Well done	20–25 minutes

Use these times as a guideline, but remember that cooking times will vary depending on how the meat has been aged and stored, the shape and thickness of the joint and personal taste. Ovens vary as well. If a recipe gives a different oven temperature, follow the recipe for timing.

How to tell if lamb is cooked

To check if roast lamb is cooked as you like it, insert a thin skewer into the centre and press out some juices: the pinker the juice that runs out, the rarer the meat.

Resting

When the lamb is cooked, cover loosely with foil and leave to rest for 20 minutes before carving. Larger joints can rest for up to 45 minutes without getting cold.

Carving leg of lamb

There are two ways to carve a leg of lamb. The first gives slices with a section of the crust; the second starts with slices that are well done and which then get progressively rarer.

Leg of lamb: method 1

1. Hold the shank and cut from that end, holding the knife flat on the bone, a couple of inches into the meat. Cut down on to the bone to remove that chunk and slice thinly.
2. Start cutting thin slices from the meat on the bone, starting at the cut left by the chunk you removed. Hold the knife at right angles to the bone, then cut at a slight angle as you reach the thicker sections of meat.
3. When you have taken off all the meat you can on that side, turn the leg and continue slicing at an angle until all the meat is removed.

Leg of lamb: method 2

1. Hold the shank with the meatiest part of the leg facing up. Slice with the knife blade parallel to the bone. When you reach the bone, turn the leg over and continue slicing (knife blade parallel to the bone) until you reach the bone.
2. Remove the remainder of the meat from both sides in single pieces and slice thinly.

Roast Spiced Leg of Lamb

Hands-on time: 25 minutes, plus minimum overnight and up to 24 hours marinating
Cooking time: 2¼ hours

1.6–1.8kg (3½–4lb) leg of lamb

2 tbsp each cumin seeds and coriander seeds

50g (2oz) blanched or flaked almonds

1 medium onion, chopped

6 garlic cloves, roughly chopped

2.5cm (1in) piece fresh root ginger, peeled and grated

4 hot green chillies, seeded and chopped (see Safety Tip, opposite)

500g carton natural yogurt

½ tsp each cayenne pepper and garam masala

3½ tsp salt

4 tbsp vegetable oil

½ tsp whole cloves, 16 cardamom pods, 1 cinnamon stick, 10 black peppercorns

fresh flat-leafed parsley sprigs to garnish

1   Put the lamb into a large shallow ceramic dish and put to one side. Put the cumin and coriander seeds into a pan and cook over a high heat until aromatic. Grind to a fine powder in a mortar and pestle. Put to one side.

2   Put the almonds, onion, garlic, ginger, chillies and 3 tbsp of the yogurt into a food processor and blend to a paste. Put the remaining yogurt into a bowl, stir well and add the paste, ground cumin and coriander, cayenne pepper, garam masala and salt. Stir well.

3   Spoon the yogurt mixture over the lamb and use a brush to push it into all the nooks and crannies. Turn the lamb, making sure it is well coated, then cover and leave to marinate in the fridge for 24 hours.

4   Take the lamb out of the fridge 1 hour before roasting to let it come up to room temperature. Preheat the oven to 200°C (180°C fan oven) mark 6. Put the lamb and marinade into a roasting tin. Heat the oil in a small frying pan, add the cloves, cardamom pods, cinnamon stick and peppercorns and fry until they begin to release their aromas. Pour over the lamb. Cover the roasting tin

with foil and roast for 1½ hours. Remove the foil and roast for a further 45 minutes, basting occasionally.

5   Transfer the lamb to a serving dish. Pick the spices out of the tin to use as a garnish. Press the sauce through a fine sieve into a bowl. Garnish the lamb with the spices and parsley and serve the sauce on the side.

Serves 6

Roast Leg of Lamb with Rosemary

Hands-on time: 15 minutes
Cooking time: 1½ hours, plus resting

2.5kg (5½ lb) leg of lamb
4 rosemary sprigs
½ tbsp oil
4 garlic cloves, cut into slivers
4 anchovy fillets, roughly chopped
4 oregano sprigs
1 large onion, thickly sliced
1 lemon, cut into 6 wedges
salt and ground black pepper
vegetables to serve

1 Take the lamb out of the fridge 1 hour before roasting. Pat the skin dry with kitchen paper.

2 Preheat the oven to 220°C (200°C fan oven) mark 7. Cut the rosemary into smaller sprigs. Rub the oil over the lamb. Cut small slits all over the meat, then insert the garlic slivers, rosemary sprigs, anchovy pieces and the leaves from two oregano sprigs into the gaps. Season well.

3 Put the onion slices into the bottom of a roasting tin just large enough to hold the lamb. Top with the remaining oregano, then put in the meat, fat side up (the onions must be covered to prevent them burning). Tuck lemon wedges around the meat.

4 Put the lamb into the oven and reduce the oven temperature to 190°C (170°C fan oven) mark 5. Roast for 15 minutes per 450lb (1lb) for pink meat, or longer if you like it more cooked.

5 Transfer the lamb to a board, cover with foil and leave to rest for 30 minutes before carving. Carefully pour (or skim) off the fat from a corner of the roasting tin, leaving the sediment behind. Put the tin on the hob over a medium heat and pour in 300–450ml (½ –¾ pint) vegetable water (or meat stock). Stir thoroughly, scraping up the sediment, and boil steadily until the gravy is a rich brown colour. Serve the lamb with the gravy and vegetables.

Prepare the lamb to the end of step 3 up to 2 hours ahead. To use, complete the recipe. The lamb is served pink here, but allow an extra 20–30 minutes if you prefer your meat more cooked.

Serves 8

Roast Lamb with Harissa

Hands-on time: 40 minutes
Cooking time: about 2 hours, plus resting

1.8kg (4lb) boned leg of lamb, plus bones, at room temperature

2 tbsp olive oil

1 bunch of fresh rosemary

1 bunch of fresh thyme

350g (12oz) shallots, peeled, root left intact and blanched

1 head of garlic, broken up into cloves, skin left on

300ml (½ pint) dry white wine

600ml (1 pint) lamb or chicken stock (see page 155)

salt and freshly ground black pepper

grilled chillies to garnish (optional)

couscous sprinkled with freshly chopped coriander to serve

For the harissa

2 large red peppers (total weight about 400g/14oz)

4 large fresh red chillies, seeded and roughly chopped (see Safety Tip, page 79)

6 garlic cloves

1 tbsp each ground coriander and caraway seeds

2 tsp salt

4 tbsp olive oil

1   To make the harissa, preheat the grill. Grill the peppers until the skins are completely blackened and the flesh is soft, then cover and leave to cool. Peel off the skins, then remove the cores and seeds. Put the chillies into a food processor with the garlic, coriander and caraway seeds and blend to a paste. Add the peppers, salt and oil and blend for 1–2 minutes until smooth.

2   To prepare the lamb, spread the bone cavity with about 3 tbsp of the harissa. Roll and secure with cocktail sticks or sew up using a trussing needle and thread.

3   Preheat the oven to 200°C (180°C fan oven) mark 6. Heat the oil in a roasting tin on the hob and brown the lamb on all sides. Season, place the

rosemary and thyme under the lamb and add the bones to the roasting tin. Roast for 1 hour for pink lamb or 1½ hours for well-done. Baste from time to time and add the shallots and garlic to the roasting tin 45 minutes before the end of the cooking time.

4 Transfer the lamb to a carving plate with the shallots and garlic. Cover loosely with foil and leave to rest in the oven at a low temperature.

5 Tilt the roasting tin and skim off any fat. Put the tin on the hob over a medium heat. Add the wine, bring to the boil and bubble until reduced by half. Add the stock, bring to the boil again and bubble until reduced by half. Season, then strain.

6 Remove the cocktail sticks or thread from the lamb and slice. Garnish with chillies, if you like. Serve with the shallots, garlic, gravy and couscous.

Serves 6

How to Butterfly a Leg of Lamb

Removing the bone makes a tender, easy-to-carve joint.

1. Place the leg of lamb on a board with the meaty side facing down and the bone facing up. With the thick end facing towards you, see if the chunky end of the pelvic bone is in place. If it is, cut it out by working all around it with a boning knife – always cutting towards the bone – then pull or twist it out.

2. Cut a long slit right down to the bone, starting from the thin end, until you reach the joint. Then scrape and cut the meat from the bone, pulling it back with your fingers, until the bone is fully exposed.

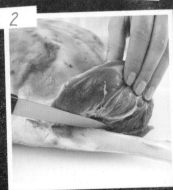

3 Work the knife carefully around the bone, cutting away from the meat, to loosen it. Twist out the bone, then follow the same procedure with the other bone.

4 Flatten the meat with your hands. Holding one hand flat on the top of the thickest part, make a cut parallel with the chopping board about midway through. Cut to within 2.5cm (1in) of the edge, then fold the meat out as if opening a book. Repeat with the other thick part of the leg and fold out.

Garlic, Lemon and Thyme Butterflied Lamb

Hands-on time: 20 minutes, plus overnight marinating
Cooking time: about 1½ hours, plus resting

2.3kg/5lb leg of lamb, boned

175ml (6fl oz) extra virgin olive oil, plus extra to brush

1 tbsp dried oregano

3 tbsp fresh thyme leaves

2 tbsp freshly chopped flat-leafed parsley

6 garlic cloves, finely chopped

150ml (¼ pint) balsamic vinegar

grated zest and juice of 2 small lemons

roast potatoes and green vegetables or cherry tomatoes and mixed leaf salad to serve

1 Open out the meat, lay skin side down and trim away any excess fat. Make slits all over it to help the marinade penetrate the flesh. Put the lamb into a ceramic dish large enough to hold it in a single layer. Whisk the oil, herbs, garlic, vinegar, lemon zest and juice together in a small bowl and pour over the meat, rubbing well into the slits. Cover and leave to marinate overnight in the fridge.

2 Remove the lamb from the fridge 1 hour before cooking to let it come up to room temperature. Preheat the oven to 220°C (200°C fan oven) mark 7. Lift the lamb from the marinade (putting the marinade to one side) and roast for 20 minutes, then reduce the oven temperature to 190°C (170°C fan oven) mark 5 and roast for a further 1 hour 10 minutes, basting with the reserved marinade from time to time, or until the meat is cooked but still slightly pink in the centre.

3 Transfer the lamb to a board and cover loosely with foil. Leave to rest for 10 minutes before carving. Serve with potatoes and vegetables or cherry tomatoes and salad.

Serves 8

Perfect Rack of Lamb

A rack of lamb comprises the seven or eight cutlets – chops from the neck end – served as a joint. Another name for rack of lamb is best end of neck of lamb. Many butchers sell it ready-trimmed, as a French-style rack, but if you need to trim it yourself, here's how.

1. If necessary, pull off the papery outer membrane from the fat side of the rack. Trim away the excess fat. Look for a long strip of cartilage on one end of the rack and cut it out if it is there. Do the same with a long strip of sinew running the length of the rack under the ribs.

2. Make a cut right down to the bone across the fat side of the rack about 2.5–5cm (1–2in) from the tips of the bones. Place the knife in that cut and, holding the knife almost parallel to the ribs, slice off the meat as a single piece to expose the ends of the bones.

3 Insert the knife between one pair of bared ribs at the point of the initial cut. Push through it to cut the meat between the ribs. Continue in the same way with the other ribs.

4 Slice down on both sides of each rib to remove the strips of meat. When you've finished, turn the rack bone side up and scrape off the papery membranes from the backs of the ribs. This will leave the top parts of the bones clean.

Roasting rack of lamb

A rack of lamb should always be cooked at a fairly high temperature so that it browns well without overcooking the eye meat. Preheat the oven to 220°C (200°C fan oven) mark 7 and cook for 25–30 minutes. If you are cooking a single rack, an alternative is to brown the fat side first; this means that you can cook it at a lower temperature, 180°C (160°C fan oven) mark 4.

Rack of Lamb with Balsamic Gravy

Hands-on time: 5 minutes
Cooking time: about 45 minutes, plus resting

4 fat garlic cloves, crushed

2 tbsp herbes de Provence

6 tbsp balsamic vinegar

12 tbsp olive oil

4 trimmed racks of lamb

salt and freshly ground black pepper

1 Preheat the oven to 220°C (200°C fan oven) mark 7. Put the garlic into a bowl with the herbs, 2 tbsp of the vinegar and 4 tbsp of the oil. Season with salt and ground black pepper.

2 Put the lamb into a roasting tin and rub the garlic mixture into both the fat and meat. Roast for 25–30 minutes if you like the meat pink, or cook for a further 5–10 minutes if you like it well done. Transfer the lamb to a warmed serving dish, cover loosely with foil and leave to rest for 10 minutes.

3 Put the roasting tin on the hob over a medium heat and whisk in the remaining vinegar and oil, scraping up any sediment as the liquid bubbles. Pour the gravy into a small jug.

4 Slice the lamb into cutlets and serve with the gravy.

Serves 8

Couscous-crusted Lamb

Hands-on time: 15 minutes
Cooking time: about 20 minutes, plus resting

75g (3oz) couscous

3 trimmed racks of lamb, excess fat trimmed off

25g (1oz) each dried cranberries and pistachios, finely chopped

2 medium eggs

1½ tsp wholegrain mustard

1½ tsp dried mint

salt and freshly ground black pepper

1 Put the couscous into a bowl and pour 125ml (4fl oz) boiling water over it. Cover with clingfilm and leave for 10 minutes.

2 Meanwhile, pat the lamb racks dry and put on to a baking tray.

3 Preheat the oven to 200°C (180°C fan oven) mark 6. Use a fork to fluff up the couscous, then stir in the cranberries, pistachios, eggs, mustard, mint and some seasoning. Press a third of the crust on top of the meat on each lamb rack.

4 Cook the lamb for 15-20 minutes for pink meat, or longer if you prefer. Transfer the racks to a board, cover loosely with foil and leave to rest for 5 minutes before carving and serving.

FREEZE AHEAD

To make ahead and freeze, prepare the lamb to the end of step 3 up to one month ahead. Wrap the baking tray well in clingfilm, then freeze. To serve, thaw the lamb overnight in the fridge, then unwrap and complete step 4 to finish the recipe.

Serves 6

Moroccan Roasted Rack of Lamb

Hands-on time: 10 minutes
Cooking time: about 25 minutes, plus resting

---

1 large bunch of fresh coriander

75g (3oz) pinenuts, fried in 1 tbsp olive oil

1 garlic clove, crushed

2 trimmed racks of lamb

2 tbsp harissa

salt and freshly ground black pepper

Saffron Couscous to serve (see below)

1 Put six coriander sprigs for the garnish to one side and chop the rest roughly. Put the coriander, pinenuts and garlic into a mini food processor and blend to a coarse paste, or crush with a pestle and mortar.

2 Season the lamb and smear the curved side of each rack with the harissa. Press the pinenut and coriander mixture on top of the harissa. Cover and chill until needed.

3 Preheat the oven to 200°C (180°C fan oven) mark 6. Put the lamb into a roasting tin and roast for 20–25 minutes until the meat is just cooked and tender, yet slightly pink. Slice each rack into cutlets and serve with couscous, garnished with the reserved coriander.

Saffron Couscous

Put 225g (8oz) couscous and 75g (3oz) raisins into a large bowl. Add a large pinch of saffron, ½ tsp salt and plenty of ground black pepper. Pour 250ml (9fl oz) hot vegetable stock over, stir, cover and leave for 10 minutes to allow the couscous to swell and absorb the liquid. To serve, stir in 25g (1oz) toasted flaked almonds.

Guard of Honour with Hazelnut and Herb Crust

Hands-on time: 30 minutes
Cooking time: about 45 minutes, plus resting

2 trimmed racks of lamb
salt and freshly ground black pepper
roasted root vegetables to serve

For the hazelnut and herb crust
75g (3oz) fresh breadcrumbs made from
    Italian bread, such as ciabatta
2 tbsp each freshly chopped flat-leafed
    parsley and thyme
1 tbsp freshly chopped rosemary
2 garlic cloves, crushed
2 tbsp olive oil
50g (2oz) hazelnuts, toasted and
    roughly chopped
4 tbsp Dijon mustard

1   Preheat the oven to 200°C (180°C fan
    oven) mark 6. Trim off as much of the
    fat from the lamb as possible and put
    to one side. Season the lamb well with
    ground black pepper.

2   Heat the reserved fat in a large
    heavy-based frying pan, add the
    lamb and sear on both sides. Remove
    the lamb from the pan and leave until
    cool enough to handle. Put the racks
    together so that the ribs interlock.
    Place the lamb in a roasting tin, rib
    bones uppermost, with the lamb fat.
    Roast for 10 minutes.

3   Meanwhile, make the hazelnut crust.
    Combine the breadcrumbs, herbs,
    garlic, oil and seasoning for 30
    seconds in a food processor, then add
    the hazelnuts and pulse for a further
    30 seconds.

4   Remove the lamb from the oven
    and spread the fatty side with the
    mustard. Press the hazelnut crust on
    to the mustard.

5 Baste the lamb with the fat in the roasting tin and put back in the oven for 15–20 minutes for rare, 20–25 minutes for medium-rare and 25–30 minutes for well done. When cooked, remove from the oven, cover loosely with foil and leave in a warm place for 10 minutes before carving. Arrange the lamb on a serving dish and serve with roasted root vegetables.

SAVE TIME

Prepare the lamb to the end of step 4. Cool quickly and chill for up to 24 hours. To use, bring the lamb to room temperature, then complete step 5 to finish the recipe.

Serves 6

Herb Lamb Cutlets

Hands-on time: 10 minutes
Cooking time: about 14 minutes

12 lamb cutlets

1½ tbsp Dijon mustard

a large handful of fresh parsley, chopped

a large handful of fresh mint, chopped

salt and freshly ground black pepper

boiled new potatoes and a salad to serve

1 Preheat the grill to medium-high. Brush the lamb cutlets with mustard and sprinkle a little seasoning over them.

2 Mix the parsley with the mint in a small bowl, then tip on to a plate. Dip each side of the lamb cutlets in the herbs, then put on to a non-stick baking sheet.

3 Grill the cutlets for 10–14 minutes (depending on the thickness and how you prefer your meat cooked), turning once. Serve with boiled new potatoes and salad.

SAVE EFFORT

Use any combination of chopped fresh herbs you like – coriander, chives and rosemary all work well.

Serves 4

Perfect Beef

Classic Roast Beef with Yorkshire Puddings

Hands-on time: 20 minutes
Cooking time: about 2 hours, plus resting

1 boned and rolled rib, sirloin, rump or topside of beef (weight about 1.8kg/4lb) at room temperature

1 tbsp plain flour

1 tbsp mustard powder

salt and freshly ground black pepper

fresh thyme sprigs to garnish

Yorkshire Puddings (see opposite) and vegetables to serve

For the gravy

150ml (¼ pint) red wine

600ml (1 pint) beef stock

1 Preheat the oven to 230°C (210°C fan oven) mark 8. Put the beef into a roasting tin, with the thickest part of the fat uppermost. Mix the flour with the mustard powder, salt and ground black pepper. Rub the mixture over the beef.

2 Roast the beef in the middle of the oven for 30 minutes.

3 Baste the beef and reduce the oven temperature to 190°C (170°C fan oven) mark 5. Cook for about 1 hour more, basting occasionally. Meanwhile, prepare the Yorkshire pudding batter (see opposite).

4 Transfer the beef to a warmed carving dish, cover loosely with foil and leave to rest in a warm place. Increase the oven temperature to 220°C (200°C fan oven) mark 7 and cook the Yorkshire Puddings.

5 Meanwhile, make the gravy. Skim off any remaining fat from the roasting tin. Put the tin on the hob over a high heat, add the wine and boil until syrupy. Pour in the stock, bring to the boil and, again, boil until syrupy; there should be about 450ml (¾ pint) gravy. Taste and adjust the seasoning.

6 Carve the beef into slices. Garnish with thyme and serve with the gravy, Yorkshire Puddings and vegetables of your choice.

Yorkshire Puddings

Sift 125g (4oz) plain flour and ½ tsp salt into a bowl. Mix in 150ml (¼ pint) milk, then add 2 medium eggs, beaten, and season with ground black pepper. Beat until smooth, then whisk in another 150ml (¼ pint) milk. Pour about 3 tbsp fat from the beef roasting tin and use to grease 8–12 individual Yorkshire pudding tins. Put the tins into a preheated oven at 220°C (200°C fan oven) mark 7 for 5 minutes or until the fat is almost smoking. Pour the batter into the tins. Bake for 15–20 minutes until well risen, golden and crisp. Serve immediately.

Serves 8

Roast Rolled Sirloin of Beef with Port Gravy

Hands-on time: 20 minutes, plus marinating
Cooking time: about 50 minutes – 1½ hours (depending on thickness of meat), plus resting

1.5–2kg (3¼–4½lb) rolled beef sirloin joint

4 fresh rosemary sprigs, leaves removed and finely chopped

2 garlic cloves, finely chopped

2 tbsp olive oil

salt and freshly ground black pepper

For the gravy

2 tbsp plain flour

400ml (14fl oz) beef stock

100ml (3½fl oz) port

1 tbsp redcurrant jelly

1 Weigh the beef and calculate the cooking time, allowing 5–15 minutes per 450g (1lb) depending on how well you like it cooked (rare to well done). Put the beef into a roasting tin just large enough to hold the joint. Mix the rosemary with the garlic, oil and lots of seasoning. Rub the mixture over the joint, then cover with clingfilm or foil and leave to marinate for 1–3 hours.

2 When the beef has marinated, preheat the oven to 200°C (180°C fan oven) mark 6. Roast the beef for 20 minutes, then reduce the oven temperature to 180°C (160°C fan oven) mark 4 and cook for your calculated time.

3 When the beef is cooked to your liking, transfer to a board, cover loosely with foil and leave to rest for 30 minutes.

4 To make the gravy, tilt the roasting tin and spoon out most of the fat. Put the tin on the hob over a medium heat and stir in the flour. Cook for 1 minute, mixing well, then gradually mix in the stock. Bubble for 3 minutes, stirring occasionally, then pour in the port. Scrape the bottom of the tin to release the sticky bits and simmer for 5 minutes. Stir in the redcurrant jelly

until dissolved, then strain through a fine sieve into a clean pan. Check the seasoning.

5 Reheat the gravy and serve with the roast beef.

SAVE TIME

Prepare the beef to the end of step 1 up to one day ahead. Cover and chill. Take the beef out of the fridge 40 minutes before roasting to allow it to come up to room temperature, then complete the recipe.

Serves 6–8

Perfect Cold Roast Beef

TAKE 5

🍴 **Hands-on time:** 15 minutes, plus overnight chilling
Cooking time: about 2 hours

2kg (4½lb) rolled topside of beef at room temperature

2 tbsp light brown soft sugar

1 tbsp mustard powder

1 tbsp vegetable oil

coleslaw, watercress leaves and creamed horseradish to serve

1 Preheat the oven to 200°C (180°C fan oven) mark 6. Pat the beef dry with kitchen paper and take a note of its weight (just in case). Mix the sugar and mustard powder in a small bowl and rub over the beef. Heat the oil in a large frying pan over a high heat and fry the beef on all sides, until well browned.

2 Sit the beef in a roasting tin just large enough to hold the joint and cover loosely with foil. Roast in the oven for 15 minutes per 500g (1lb 2oz) for rare meat, 20 minutes per 500g (1lb 2oz) for medium-rare meat or 25 minutes per 500g (1lb 2oz) for well-done meat, then roast for an extra 10 minutes on top of the calculated time. Or use a meat thermometer – for medium-rare meat the internal temperature of the beef should be 60°C.

3 Transfer the beef to a board and leave to cool completely. Wrap well in foil and chill in the fridge overnight. (You can also serve this beef hot as part of a Sunday lunch – just leave it to rest for 30 minutes after roasting, then carve.)

4 An hour before serving, slice the beef thinly and arrange on a platter, then cover. Serve with coleslaw, watercress leaves and creamed horseradish.

SAVE TIME

Cook the beef to the end of step 3 up to three days ahead, then complete the recipe and chill.

Serves 8

Beef Rib with Mustard, Parsley and Onion Crust

Hands-on time: 20 minutes
Cooking time: about 2 hours, plus resting

1 large onion, finely chopped

150ml (¼ pint) red wine or dry sherry

2.3kg (5lb) boned and rolled rib of beef at room temperature

2 tbsp English mustard

2 tbsp freshly chopped flat-leafed parsley

salt and freshly ground black pepper

roasted root vegetables and green vegetables to serve

SAVE TIME

Prepare the onion mixture to the end of step 1, then cool, cover and chill for up to 24 hours. Complete steps 2, 3 and 4 to finish the recipe.

1 Preheat the oven to 240°C (220°C fan oven) mark 9. Put the onion into a frying pan with the wine or sherry. Bring to the boil and bubble gently until most of the liquid has evaporated, then leave to cool.

2 Put the beef into a large roasting tin and season all over with ground black pepper. Roast (with no extra fat) for 30 minutes. Reduce the oven temperature to 190°C (170°C fan oven) mark 5 and continue to cook for 15 minutes per 450g (1lb) for rare, plus 15 minutes extra for medium-rare or 30 minutes extra for well-done meat.

3 About 10 minutes before the beef is cooked, transfer the joint to a smaller tin, keeping the large tin containing all the juices for the gravy (see page 158). Smear the mustard all over the beef. Add the parsley to the cooled onion mixture, season with salt and ground black pepper and press on

to the beef. Put back in the oven to finish cooking.

4 Transfer the cooked beef to a warmed carving dish, cover loosely with foil and leave to rest for 30 minutes before serving. Carve the meat into slices and serve with roasted root vegetables and green vegetables.

Serves 6

Perfect Preparation

Follow these tried and tested instructions
for trimming a joint, tying and larding.

Trimming

1 Cut off the excess fat to leave a
thickness of about 5mm (¼in).
This isn't necessary for very
lean cuts.

2 Trim away any stray pieces of
meat or sinew left by the butcher.

3 If the joint has a covering of fat,
you can lightly score it – taking
care not to cut into the meat –
to help the fat drain away
during cooking.

Tying

Tie the joint if you are using a boned and rolled joint, or if you have boned the joint but want to roast it using the bones as a 'roasting rack'.

1 Tie a piece of string around the length of the joint, securing it to the bones if you are using them. If you are cooking a boned and rolled joint, turn it 90 degrees, then tie another piece in the same way.

2 Starting at one end of the joint, loop string around the meat and tie it securely and firmly. Cut it off and make another loop about 5cm (2in) from the first.

3 Continue tying the joint in this way along the whole length of the joint until it is neatly and firmly secured.

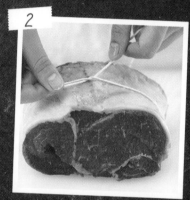

Larding

Threading narrow strips of fat through lean joints of beef helps to ensure juiciness. The fat is threaded through the joint using a larding needle (available from specialist kitchen stores).

1 Cut long strips of pork fat, preferably back fat, which will fit easily into the larding needle.

2 Push the needle right through the joint, so that the tip sticks out at least 5cm (2in) through the other side.

3 Take a strip of fat, place it in the hollow of the larding needle and feed it into the tip. When the fat can't go in any further, press down on the joint and pull the needle out. The fat should stay inside.

4 Repeat at 2.5cm (1in) intervals all around the joint.

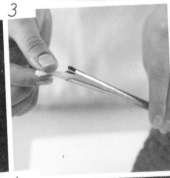

Larding tips

❑ Larding is much easier if the strips of fat are very cold or even frozen
❑ The strips of fat don't need to be as long as the joint: you can put several pieces of fat in a single larding channel
❑ Use one strip per 2.5cm (1in), measuring the longer side of the joint

Beef roasting times

Preheat the oven to 220°C (200°C fan oven) mark 7. Weigh the joint to calculate the roasting time. Brown the beef in the hot oven for 20 minutes, then turn the oven down to 190°C (170°C fan oven) mark 5 and roast for the calculated time.

	COOKING TIME PER 450G (1LB)
Rare	15 minutes
Medium	20 minutes
Well done	25 minutes

Use these times as a guideline, but remember that cooking times will vary depending on how the meat has been aged and stored, the shape and thickness of the joint, and personal taste. Ovens vary as well. If a recipe gives a different oven temperature, follow the recipe for timing.

How to tell if beef is cooked

To check if roast beef is cooked as you like it, insert a thin skewer into the centre and press out some juices. The juices that run out indicate the stage to which the beef is cooked: red juices for rare, pink for medium-rare, or clear for well done.

Resting

When the beef is cooked, cover loosely with foil and leave to rest for 30 minutes before carving. Larger joints can rest for up to 45 minutes without getting cold.

Fillet of Beef with Mushrooms and Chestnuts

Hands-on Time: 20 minutes, plus 2–3 hours marinating
Cooking Time: 45 minutes, plus resting

1kg (2¼lb) fillet of beef, trimmed
100g (3½oz) butter
350ml (12fl oz) beef or veal stock
2 tbsp mixed peppercorns, crushed
1 tbsp vegetable oil
1 medium shallot, finely chopped
450g (1lb) mixed wild mushrooms,
    cleaned and trimmed
200g (7oz) cooked and peeled (or
    vacuum-packed) chestnuts, halved
3 tbsp finely chopped flat-leafed parsley
salt and ground black pepper

For the marinade
400ml (14fl oz) red wine
50ml (2fl oz) Madeira
2 tbsp balsamic vinegar
5 large shallots, sliced
1 bay leaf and 1 fresh thyme sprig

1 Put the beef in a bowl, add the marinade ingredients, cover and leave in a cool place for 2–3 hours. Remove the shallots and beef with a slotted spoon; keep the liquid. Pat the beef dry with kitchen paper. Melt 25g (1oz) butter in a pan and gently fry the shallots. Add the marinade and boil until reduced to one-third. Add the stock and boil to reduce to one-third. Discard the bay and thyme. Set the sauce aside.

2 Preheat the oven to 200°C (180°C fan oven) mark 6. Roll the beef in the crushed peppercorns. Heat the oil in a heavy-based frying pan and brown the beef over a high heat. Put the beef in a roasting tin and roast for 25 minutes for medium-rare. Put the meat on a board, cover with foil and rest for 10 minutes.

3 Melt 25g (1oz) butter in a pan and cook the shallot until soft. Add the mushrooms and sauté until the liquid has evaporated. Stir in the chestnuts and parsley, and season. Set aside. Reheat the sauce and whisk in the remaining butter. Carve the beef and serve with the mushrooms, chestnuts and sauce.

Serves 6

Fillet of Beef en Croûte

Hands-on time: 1 hour, plus soaking and chilling
Cooking time: about 1¼ hours, plus cooling and resting

1–1.4kg (2¼–3lb) fillet of beef, trimmed

50g (2oz) butter

2 shallots, chopped

15g (½oz) dried porcini mushrooms, soaked in 100ml (3½fl oz) boiling water

2 garlic cloves, chopped

225g (8oz) flat mushrooms, finely chopped

2 tsp freshly chopped thyme, plus extra sprigs to garnish

175g (6oz) chicken liver pâté

175g (6oz) thinly sliced Parma ham

375g ready-rolled puff pastry

plain flour to dust

1 medium egg, beaten

salt and freshly ground black pepper

Red Wine Sauce to serve (see page 118)

1 Season the beef with salt and ground black pepper. Melt 25g (1oz) of the butter in a large frying pan and, when foaming, add the beef and cook for 4–5 minutes to brown all over. Transfer to a plate and leave to cool.

2 Melt the remaining butter in a pan, add the shallots and cook for 1 minute. Drain the porcini mushrooms, putting the liquid to one side, and chop them. Add them to the pan with the garlic, the reserved liquid and the fresh mushrooms. Turn up the heat and cook until the liquid has evaporated, then season with salt and pepper and add the chopped thyme. Leave to cool.

3 Put the chicken liver pâté into a bowl and beat until smooth. Add the mushroom mixture and stir well. Spread half the mushroom mixture evenly over one side of the fillet. Lay half the Parma ham on a length of clingfilm, overlapping the slices. Invert the mushroom-topped beef on to the ham. Spread the remaining mushroom mixture on the other side of the beef, then lay the rest of the Parma ham, also overlapping, on top of the mushroom mixture. Wrap the beef in the clingfilm to form a firm sausage shape and chill for 30 minutes. Preheat the oven to 220°C (200°C fan oven) mark 7.

4 Cut off one-third of the pastry and roll out on a lightly floured worksurface to 3mm (⅛in) thick and 2.5cm (1in) larger all round than the beef. Prick all over with a fork. Transfer to a baking sheet and bake for 12–15 minutes until brown and crisp. Leave to cool, then trim to the size of the beef and place on a baking sheet. Remove the clingfilm from the beef, brush with the beaten egg and place on the cooked pastry.

5 Roll out the remaining pastry to a 25.5 × 30.5cm (10 × 12in) rectangle. Roll a lattice pastry cutter over the pastry and gently ease the lattice open. Cover the beef with the lattice, tuck the ends under and seal the edges. Brush with the beaten egg, then cook for 40 minutes for rare to medium, 45 minutes for medium. Leave to rest for 10 minutes before carving. Garnish with thyme sprigs and serve with Red Wine Sauce.

Red Wine Sauce

Soften 350g (12oz) finely chopped shallots in 2 tbsp olive oil for 5 minutes. Add 3 chopped garlic cloves and 3 tbsp tomato purée and cook for 1 minute, then add 2 tbsp balsamic vinegar. Simmer briskly until reduced to almost nothing, then add 200ml (7fl oz) red wine and reduce by half. Pour in 600ml (1 pint) beef stock and bring to the boil, then reduce the heat and simmer until reduced by one-third.

Serves 6

Stuffed Topside of Beef

Hands-on time: 35 minutes, plus marinating
Cooking time: about 1½ hours, plus resting

1.4kg (3lb) topside or top rump of beef

1 tbsp balsamic vinegar

2 tbsp white wine vinegar

3 tbsp olive oil

3 tbsp freshly chopped marjoram
or thyme

2 red peppers, seeded and quartered

75g (3oz) fresh spinach, cooked and
well drained

75g (3oz) pitted black olives, chopped

50g (2oz) smoked ham, chopped

75g (3oz) raisins or sultanas

salt and freshly ground black pepper

roast potatoes and vegetables to serve

1 Make a deep cut along the beef to
create a pocket and put it into a dish.
Combine the vinegars, oil, marjoram
or thyme and some ground black
pepper. Pour over the beef and into
the pocket. Marinate in a cool place
for 4–6 hours or overnight.

2 Preheat the grill. Grill the peppers,
skin side up, under a hot grill until
the skins are charred. Put into a bowl,

cover and leave to cool, then remove
the skins.

3 Squeeze the excess water from the
spinach, then chop and put into a
bowl with the olives, ham and raisins
or sultanas. Mix well and season with
salt and ground black pepper.

4 Preheat the oven to 190°C (170°C fan
oven) mark 5. Line the pocket of the
beef with the peppers, keeping back
two pepper quarters for the gravy.
Spoon the spinach mixture into
the pocket and spread evenly.
Reshape the meat and tie at
intervals with string.

5 Put the beef into a roasting tin just
large enough to hold the joint. Pour
the marinade over and roast for 1
hour for rare, or 1¼ hours for medium-
rare, basting from time to time.
Transfer the beef to a board, cover
loosely with foil and rest in a warm
place while you make the gravy.

6 Skim off the excess fat from the
roasting tin. Put the tin on the hob

over a high heat and bring the pan juices to the boil. Add 125ml (4fl oz) water and bubble for 2-3 minutes. Finely chop the remaining pepper pieces and add to the gravy.

7 Carve the beef and serve with the gravy, roast potatoes and vegetables of your choice.

Serves 6

Spiced Silverside

Hands-on time: 20 minutes, plus soaking
Cooking time: about 5 hours, plus cooling

1.8kg (4lb) piece boned, salted silverside
1 onion, sliced
4 carrots, sliced
1 small turnip, sliced
1–2 celery sticks, chopped
8 cloves
125g (4oz) light muscovado sugar
½ tsp English mustard powder
1 tsp ground cinnamon
juice of 1 orange

1 Soak the meat for several hours or overnight in enough cold water to cover it.

2 Rinse the meat and put it into a large heavy-based pan with the vegetables. Add water to cover the meat and bring slowly to the boil. Skim off any scum, then cover with a lid, reduce the heat and simmer for 4 hours. Leave to cool in the liquid.

3 Preheat the oven to 180°C (160°C fan oven) mark 4. Drain the meat well, then put into a roasting tin and press the cloves into the fat. Mix the sugar with the mustard, cinnamon and orange juice and spread over the meat.

4 Roast for 45 minutes–1 hour, basting from time to time. Serve hot or cold.

Serves 6

Veggie Dishes

White Nut Roast

Hands-on time: 20 minutes,
Cooking time: about 1 hour plus cooling

40g (1½oz) butter, plus a little extra
    to grease

1 onion, finely chopped

1 garlic clove, crushed

225g (8oz) mixed white nuts, such as
    brazils, macadamias, pinenuts and
    whole almonds, ground in a food
    processor

125g (4oz) fresh white breadcrumbs

grated zest and juice of ½ lemon

75g (3oz) sage Derby cheese or
    Parmesan, grated (see opposite)

125g (4oz) cooked, peeled (or vacuum-
    packed) chestnuts, roughly chopped

½ × 400g can artichoke hearts, drained
    and roughly chopped

1 medium egg, lightly beaten

2 tsp each freshly chopped parsley, sage
    and thyme, plus extra sprigs

salt and freshly ground black pepper

1 Preheat the oven to 200°C (180°C fan oven) mark 6. Melt the butter in a pan and cook the onion and garlic for 5 minutes or until soft. Put into a large bowl and leave to cool.

2 Add the nuts, breadcrumbs, lemon zest and juice, cheese, chestnuts and artichokes to the cooled onion mixture. Season well and bind together with the egg. Stir in the chopped herbs.

3 Put the mixture on to a large piece of buttered foil and shape into a fat sausage, packing tightly. Scatter with the extra herb sprigs and wrap in the foil.

4 Place on a baking sheet and cook in the oven for 35 minutes, then unwrap the foil slightly and cook for a further 15 minutes or until turning golden.

Serves 8

Red Cabbage Timbales with Mushroom Stuffing

1 medium red cabbage (weight about
   1.4kg/3lb)

Mushroom and Cashew Nut Stuffing
   (see opposite)

40g (1½oz) butter

375g (13oz) onions, finely chopped

3 tbsp balsamic vinegar

salt and freshly ground black pepper

small fresh thyme sprigs to garnish
   (optional)

green vegetables to serve

For the sauce

4 tbsp caster sugar

4 tbsp red wine vinegar

150ml (¼ pint) red wine

1 tbsp lemon juice

1 Put the cabbage into a large pan of boiling water. Bring back to the boil, then reduce the heat and simmer until the outside leaves have softened enough to be eased away. Lift the cabbage out of the pan; keep the water. Remove three outer leaves and boil them for a further 3–4 minutes, then place in a bowl of cold water. Quarter the whole cabbage and remove the core. Take 700g (1½lb) of the cabbage, remove and discard any thick central vein, then shred the leaves very finely, cover and put to one side.

2 Preheat the oven to 190°C (170°C fan oven) mark 5. Line six 150ml (¼ pint) moulds with clingfilm. Drain the whole cabbage leaves and cut in half; discard the central vein. Use the leaves to line the moulds. Fill with stuffing and cover with foil. Place in a large roasting tin and pour in enough warm water to come halfway up the sides of the moulds. Cook for 30 minutes or until just set to the centre.

3 Meanwhile, melt the butter in a pan, add the onions and cook until

soft. Mix in the shredded cabbage, vinegar, 3 tbsp water and season. Cook, stirring from time to time, for 15–20 minutes until just tender.

4 To make the sauce, put the sugar and vinegar into a pan. Cook over a low heat until the sugar has dissolved, then bring to the boil and cook to a rich caramel. Pour in the wine and allow to reduce by half, then add lemon juice to taste and season. Cool.

5 Turn out the timbales, spoon shredded cabbage on top and around, drizzle the sauce over and garnish with thyme, if you like. Serve with green vegetables.

Mushroom and Cashew Nut Stuffing

Melt 50g (2oz) butter in a pan, add 200g (7oz) finely chopped onions and cook until soft and golden. Add 450g (1lb) roughly chopped chestnut mushrooms and fry over a medium heat or until the moisture has evaporated. Stir in 75g (3oz) roughly chopped salted cashew nuts, 4 tbsp freshly chopped flat-leafed parsley and 125g (4oz) fresh breadcrumbs. Leave to cool, then stir in 2 large beaten eggs and season with salt and freshly ground black pepper. Mix well, then cover and put to one side. This stuffing can also be used for chicken or turkey.

Serves 6

Roasted Stuffed Peppers

Hands-on time: 20 minutes
Cooking time: about 50 minutes

40g (1½oz) butter

4 Romano peppers, halved, with stalks
on and seeded

3 tbsp olive oil

350g (12oz) chestnut mushrooms,
roughly chopped

4 tbsp finely chopped fresh chives

100g (3½oz) feta

50g (2oz) fresh white breadcrumbs

25g (1oz) freshly grated Parmesan

salt and freshly ground black pepper

1   Preheat the oven to 180°C (160°C fan oven) mark 4. Use a little of the butter to grease a shallow ovenproof dish and put the peppers in it side by side, ready to be filled.

2   Heat the remaining butter and 1 tbsp of the oil in a pan. Add the mushrooms and fry until golden and no excess liquid is left in the pan. Stir in the chives, then spoon the mixture into the pepper halves.

3   Crumble the feta over the mushrooms. Mix the breadcrumbs and Parmesan in a bowl, then sprinkle over the peppers. Season with salt and ground black pepper and drizzle with the remaining oil.

4   Roast in the oven for 45 minutes or until golden and tender. Serve warm.

SAVE TIME

Complete the recipe up to one day ahead, then cover and chill. To serve, reheat under the grill for 5 minutes.

Serves 8

Baked Stuffed Pumpkin

Hands-on time: about 40 minutes
Cooking time: about 1 hour 50 minutes, plus standing

1 pumpkin (weight about 1.4–1.8kg/ 3–4lb)

2 tbsp olive oil

2 leeks, trimmed and chopped

2 garlic cloves, crushed

2 tbsp freshly chopped thyme leaves

2 tsp paprika

1 tsp ground turmeric

125g (4oz) long-grain rice, cooked

2 tomatoes, peeled, seeded and diced

50g (2oz) cashew nuts, toasted and roughly chopped

125g (4oz) Cheddar, grated

salt and freshly ground black pepper

1 Cut a 5cm (2in) slice from the top of the pumpkin and put to one side for the lid. Scoop out and discard the seeds. Using a knife and a spoon, cut out most of the pumpkin flesh, leaving a thin shell. Cut the flesh into small pieces and put to one side.

2 Heat the oil in a large pan, add the leeks, garlic, thyme, paprika and turmeric and fry for 10 minutes. Add the chopped pumpkin flesh and fry for a further 10 minutes or until golden, stirring frequently to prevent sticking. Transfer the mixture to a bowl. Preheat the oven to 180°C (160°C fan oven) mark 4.

3 Add the pumpkin mixture to the cooked rice along with the tomatoes, cashews and cheese. Fork through to mix and season with salt and ground black pepper.

4 Spoon the stuffing mixture into the pumpkin shell, top with the lid and bake for 1¼–1½ hours until the pumpkin is softened and the skin is browned. Remove from the oven and leave to stand for 10 minutes. Cut into wedges to serve.

Sweet Roasted Fennel

Hands-on time: 10 minutes
Cooking time: about 1 hour

700g (1½lb) fennel (about 3 bulbs)

3 tbsp olive oil

50g (2oz) butter, melted

1 lemon, halved

1 tsp caster sugar

2 large fresh thyme sprigs

salt and freshly ground black pepper

1 Preheat the oven to 200°C (180°C fan oven) mark 6. Trim and quarter the fennel and put into a large roasting tin.

2 Drizzle the fennel with the oil and melted butter and squeeze the lemon juice over. Add the lemon halves to the roasting tin. Sprinkle with sugar and season generously with salt and ground black pepper. Add the thyme and cover with a damp piece of non-stick baking parchment.

3 Roast for 30 minutes, then remove the baking parchment and cook for a further 20–30 minutes until lightly charred and tender.

Serves 4

Roasted Butternut Squash

Hands-on time: 15 minutes
Cooking time: 40 minutes

2 butternut squash
2 tbsp olive oil
25g (1oz) butter
2 tbsp freshly chopped thyme leaves
1 red chilli, seeded and finely chopped
  (see Safety Tip, page 79)
salt and freshly ground black pepper

1 Preheat the oven to 220°C (200°C fan oven) mark 7. Cut the squash in half lengthways and scoop out the seeds. Cut in half again, then put into a roasting tin. Drizzle with the oil, season with salt and ground black pepper and roast for 40 minutes.

2 Meanwhile, put the butter into a bowl with the thyme and chilli and mix well. Add a little to each slice of cooked butternut squash.

SAVE EFFORT

For an easy alternative flavour, use crushed garlic instead of chilli.

136

Sage-roasted Parsnips, Apples and Prunes

Hands-on time: 20 minutes
Cooking time: about 55 minutes

6–8 tbsp olive oil

1.8kg (4lb) parsnips, peeled, quartered and cored

6 apples, peeled, quartered and cored

16 ready-to-eat prunes

50g (2oz) butter

1–2 tbsp freshly chopped sage leaves

1–2 tbsp runny honey (optional)

salt and freshly ground black pepper

1   Heat 3–4 tbsp of the oil in a large roasting tin, add the parsnips in batches and fry over a medium heat until a rich golden brown all over. Remove from the tin and put to one side. Add 3–4 tbsp of the oil to the same tin and fry the apples until golden brown. Remove from the tin and put to one side.

2   Preheat the oven to 200°C (180°C fan oven) mark 6. Put the parsnips back into the tin, season with salt and ground black pepper and roast for 15 minutes.

3   Add the apples and continue roasting for 10 minutes. Put the prunes into the tin and roast for a further 5 minutes. At the end of this time, test the apples. If they are still firm, roast everything for a further 5–10 minutes until the apples are soft and fluffy.

4   Put the tin on the hob over a very low heat. Add the butter and sage, drizzle with honey, if you like, and spoon into a hot serving dish.

SAVE TIME

Prepare the parsnips and apples to the end of step 1, then cool, cover and chill for up to one day. Complete steps 2, 3 and 4 to finish the recipe.

Serves 8

Sides, Sauces and Gravies

Roasted Mediterranean Vegetables

Hands-on time: 10 minutes
Cooking time: about 40 minutes

4 plum tomatoes, halved

2 onions, quartered

4 red peppers, seeded and cut into strips

2 courgettes, cut into thick slices

4 garlic cloves, unpeeled

6 tbsp olive oil

1 tbsp freshly chopped thyme leaves

sea salt flakes and freshly ground
   black pepper

1 Preheat the oven to 220°C (200°C fan oven) mark 7. Put the tomatoes into a large roasting tin with the onions, peppers, courgettes and garlic. Drizzle with the oil and sprinkle with thyme, sea salt and ground black pepper.

2 Roast, turning occasionally, for 35-40 minutes until tender.

HEALTHY TIP

To make a nutritionally complete meal, sprinkle with toasted sesame seeds and serve with hummus.

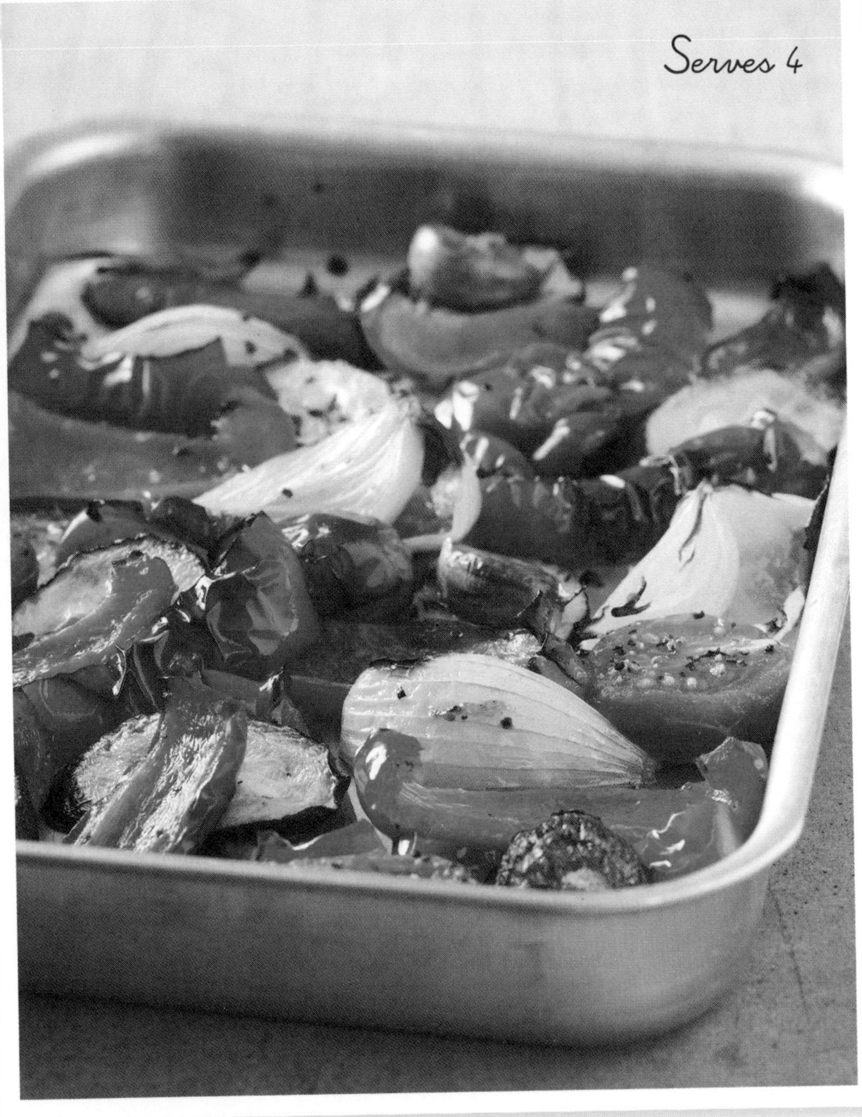
Serves 4

Mustard-roasted Potatoes and Parsnips

TAKE 5

🍴 **Hands-on time:** 25 minutes
Cooking time: about 1¼ hours

1.4kg (3lb) small even-sized potatoes, scrubbed

800g (1lb 12oz) small parsnips, peeled

50g (2oz) goose fat

1-2 tbsp black mustard seeds

1 tbsp sea salt

1 Cut out small wedges from one side of each of the potatoes and parsnips (this will help make them extra crispy). Put them into a pan of salted cold water, bring to the boil and cook for 6 minutes. Drain well.

2 Preheat the oven to 200°C (180°C fan oven) mark 6. Heat the goose fat in a roasting tin for 4-5 minutes until sizzling hot. Add the potatoes, toss in the fat and roast for 30 minutes. Add the parsnips and sprinkle with the mustard seeds and sea salt. Roast for a further 30-35 minutes, turning after 20 minutes, until the vegetables are golden.

FREEZE AHEAD

Prepare the vegetables to the end of step 1. Spread them out on a baking tray and leave to cool, then freeze on the tray. Once frozen, put them into a plastic bag and freeze for up to three months. To use, cook from frozen, allowing an additional 15-20 minutes total cooking time.

Serves 8

Roast Baby Potatoes

Hands-on time: 3 minutes
Cooking time: about 35 minutes

1kg (2¼ lb) baby potatoes

2 tbsp olive oil

salt and freshly ground black pepper

1 Preheat the oven to 220°C (200°C fan oven) mark 7. Empty the potatoes into a roasting tin and drizzle the oil over. Season well and toss gently to mix everything together.

2 Roast the potatoes for 30–35 minutes, tossing occasionally, until tender. Serve immediately.

SAVE EFFORT

Prepare the potatoes to the end of step 1 up to 3 hours ahead. Cover and store at cool room temperature. Complete step 2 to serve.

Serves 6

Spiced Red Cabbage

Hands-on time: 10 minutes
Cooking time: about 15 minutes

1 tbsp olive oil

15g (½oz) butter

½–1 tsp each ground ginger and coriander

½ medium red cabbage (weight about 450g/1lb), finely shredded

2 tbsp balsamic vinegar

1 tbsp caster sugar

a large handful of fresh curly parsley, roughly chopped

salt and freshly ground black pepper

1 Heat the oil and butter in a large pan over a high heat. Stir in the spices and cook for 1 minute. Add the cabbage and cook for 10 minutes, stirring often, or until just softened.

2 Pour in the vinegar and sugar and cook for 3 minutes. Stir in the parsley and check the seasoning. Serve immediately.

SAVE TIME

Complete steps 1 and 2 without adding the parsley up to 3 hours ahead. Cover and chill. To serve, reheat gently in a pan and complete the recipe.

Roasted Root Vegetables

Hands-on time: 15 minutes
Cooking time: about 1 hour

1 large potato, cut into large chunks
1 large sweet potato, cut into
  large chunks
3 carrots, cut into large chunks
4 small parsnips, halved lengthways
1 small swede, cut into large chunks
3 tbsp olive oil
2 fresh rosemary and 2 fresh
  thyme sprigs
salt and freshly ground black pepper

1 Preheat the oven to 200°C (180°C fan oven) mark 6. Put all the vegetables into a large roasting tin. Add the oil.
2 Use scissors to snip the herbs over the vegetables, then season with salt and ground black pepper and toss everything together. Roast for 1 hour or until tender.

SAVE EFFORT

An easy way to get a brand new dish is to use other combinations of vegetables: try celeriac instead of parsnips, fennel instead of swede, peeled shallots instead of carrots.

Thyme Tomatoes

Hands-on time: 3 minutes
Cooking time: about 12 minutes

500g (1lb 2oz) cherry tomatoes, on the vine

1 tbsp olive oil

3 fresh thyme sprigs

salt and freshly ground black pepper

1 Preheat the oven to 220°C (200°C fan oven) mark 7. Trim the tomatoes into small bunches and put the bunches into a small roasting tin. Drizzle with the oil, add the thyme and season well with salt and ground black pepper.

2 Roast for 10–12 minutes until the tomatoes have burst but are still holding their shape. Remove the thyme and serve immediately.

SAVE TIME

Prepare the tomatoes to the end of step 1 up to 3 hours ahead. Cover and store at cool room temperature, then complete step 2 to serve..

Serves 6

Perfect Stock

Good stock can make the difference between a good dish and
a great one. It gives depth of flavour to many dishes.

Vegetable Stock

For 1.1 litres (2 pints), you will need:
225g (8oz) each chopped onions,
celery, leeks and carrots, 2 bay leaves,
a few thyme sprigs, 1 small bunch of
fresh parsley, 10 black peppercorns,
½ tsp salt.

1   Put all the ingredients into a large
    pan and add 1.7 litres (3 pints) cold
    water. Bring slowly to the boil and
    skim the surface.
2   Partially cover the pan, then
    reduce the heat and simmer for
    30 minutes. Adjust the seasoning
    if necessary. Strain the stock
    through a fine sieve into a bowl
    and leave to cool. Cover and chill
    in the fridge for up to three days.
    Use as required.

Basic Bone Stock

For 900ml–1.1 litres (1½–2 pints), you will need:
900g (2lb) meat bones, fresh or from cooked meat, 2 onions, chopped, 2 carrots, chopped, 1 tsp salt, 3 black peppercorns and 1 bouquet garni (1 bay leaf, a few fresh parsley and thyme sprigs).

1 Chop the bones. Put in a pan with 2 litres (3½ pints) water, the vegetables, salt, peppercorns and herbs. Bring to the boil and skim off any scum. Cover and simmer for about 3 hours. Strain the stock and, when cold, remove all traces of fat.

Chicken Stock

For 1.1 litres (2 pints), you will need:
1.6kg (3½lb) chicken bones, 225g (8oz) each onions and celery, both sliced, 150g (5oz) chopped leeks, 1 bouquet garni (2 bay leaves, a few fresh thyme sprigs and a small bunch of fresh parsley), 1 tsp black peppercorns, ½ tsp salt.

1 Put all the ingredients into a large pan and add 3 litres (5¼ pints) cold water. Bring slowly to the boil and skim the surface.
2 Partially cover the pan, then reduce the heat and simmer gently for 2 hours. Adjust the seasoning if necessary.
3 Strain the stock through a muslin-lined sieve into a bowl and cool quickly. Cover and chill in the fridge for up to three days. Use as required. Degrease (see page 156) before using.

Giblet Stock

To make 1.3 litres (2¼ pints), you will need:

turkey giblets, 1 quartered onion, 1 halved carrot, 1 halved celery stick, 6 black peppercorns, 1 bay leaf.

1 Put all the ingredients into a large pan and add 1.4 litres (2½ pints) cold water. Cover and bring to the boil.

2 Reduce the heat and simmer for 30 minutes–1 hour, skimming occasionally. Strain through a sieve into a bowl and cool quickly. Cover and chill for up to two days.

Degreasing stock

Meat and poultry stock needs to be degreased – vegetable stock does not. You can mop the fat from the surface using kitchen paper, but the following methods are easier and more effective. There are three main methods that you can use: ladling, pouring and chilling.

1 **Ladling** While the stock is warm, place a ladle on the surface. Press down and allow the fat floating on the surface to trickle over the edge until the ladle is full. Discard the fat, then repeat until all the fat has been removed.

2 **Pouring** For this you need a degreasing jug or a double-pouring gravy boat, which has the spout at the base of the vessel. When you fill the jug or gravy boat with a fatty liquid, the fat rises. When you pour, the stock comes out while the fat stays behind in the jug.

3 **Chilling** This technique works best with stock made from meat, as the fat solidifies when cold. Put the stock in the fridge until the fat becomes solid, then remove the pieces of fat using a slotted spoon.

3

Classic Gravy

Hands-on time: 2 minutes
Cooking time: 10 minutes

juices in the roasting tin

about 2 tbsp plain flour

about 1.1 litres (2 pints) stock (see
   pages 154–6)

salt and freshly ground black pepper

1 Make the gravy while the meat or poultry is resting. Tilt the roasting tin to tip the liquid into one corner. Spoon off most of the fat, leaving about 2 tbsp fat and the juices in the tin.

2 Put the roasting tin on the hob over a low heat and add the flour. Stir it in with a wooden spoon and cook for 1–2 minutes. Don't worry if it looks horribly lumpy at this point.

3 Gradually pour in the stock, whisking it in using a balloon whisk. Bring the gravy to the boil, whisking all the time, then let it bubble and reduce a little to concentrate the flavour. Taste, season and keep warm until ready to serve.

Serves 8

Take 5 Gravies

Basic Gravy

To make about 300ml (½ pint), you will need:

juices in the roasting tin, 300–450ml (½ –¾ pint) vegetable water, or chicken, vegetable or meat stock (see pages 154–6), salt and freshly ground black pepper.

1 While the meat or poultry is resting, tilt the roasting tin and carefully pour (or skim) off the fat from one corner, leaving just the dark brown juices. Put the tin on the hob over a medium heat and pour in the vegetable water or stock as appropriate.

2 Stir thoroughly, scraping up the sediment, then bring to the boil and boil steadily until the gravy is a rich brown colour. Taste, season and keep warm until ready to serve.

Thick Gravy Sprinkle 1–2 tbsp flour into the roasting tin and cook, stirring, until browned, then gradually stir in the liquid and cook, stirring, for 2–3 minutes until smooth and slightly thickened.

Rich Madeira Gravy

To serve eight, you will need:
juices in the roasting tin, 40g (1½oz)
plain flour, 150ml (¼ pint) Madeira,
about 1.1 litres (2 pints) stock (see
pages 154–6), 2 tbsp redcurrant jelly,
salt and freshly ground black pepper.

1 While the meat or poultry is
   resting, tilt the roasting tin and
   pour off as much of the fat as you
   can, leaving just the dark brown
   juices. Put the tin on the hob over
   a low heat, stir in the flour with
   a wooden spoon, then gradually
   pour in the Madeira and bubble
   for 1 minute.
2 Gradually pour in the stock
   and mix in, scraping up all the
   goodness from the bottom of the
   tin. Bring to the boil, then add the
   redcurrant jelly, reduce the heat
   and simmer for 5 minutes. Taste
   and season, then pour through a
   sieve into a sauceboat and keep
   warm until ready to serve.

Rich Red Wine Gravy

This rich gravy goes well with
roasted chicken or meat such as beef.

To serve eight, you will need:
4 tbsp plain flour, 300ml (½ pint) red
wine, 1.1 litres (2 pints) chicken or
beef stock, salt and freshly ground
black pepper.

1 While the meat or poultry is
   resting, strain the juices from the
   roasting tin into a bowl and skim
   off any fat, keeping 3 tbsp of the
   fat to one side.
2 Put the fat back into the tin and
   whisk in the flour. Cook over
   a medium heat until the flour
   browns. Take off the heat, stir in
   the wine until smooth, then bubble
   for 2–3 minutes.
3 Stir in the chicken or meat juices
   and the stock and bring to the
   boil, then bubble for 10–15 minutes
   until reduced by half and the
   gravy is smooth. Skim off any fat
   and season with salt and ground
   black pepper. Keep warm until
   ready to serve.

White Wine Gravy
Perfect served with roast chicken.

To serve eight, you will need:
4 tbsp plain flour, 500ml (18fl oz)
chicken stock (see page 155), 150ml
(¼ pint) dry white wine,
2 tbsp redcurrant jelly, salt and
freshly ground black pepper.

1 While the chicken is resting, tilt
   the roasting tin and carefully
   pour (or skim) off the fat from one
   corner, leaving just the dark brown
   juices. Spoon 3 tbsp of the juices
   into a bowl and mix with the flour
   to make a paste.

2 Pour the chicken stock, white
   wine and redcurrant jelly into the
   roasting tin and scrape the residue
   from the bottom of the tin using a
   wooden spoon.
3 Put the roasting tin on the hob
   over a low heat and whisk in the
   flour mixture. Simmer gently for
   5–10 minutes, then season to
   taste with salt and ground black
   pepper and keep warm until
   ready to serve.

Mustard and Honey Gravy

If you don't like turkey giblet stock, use good chicken stock instead. Honey helps to disguise the bitterness from over-browned turkey juices.

To serve eight, you will need: 3½ tbsp plain flour, 1½ tbsp honey, 75ml (3fl oz) white wine, 700ml (1¼ pint) hot turkey stock (see right) and ½–1tbsp wholegrain mustard.

SAVE TIME

Make the gravy up to 1 hour ahead. Strain into a small pan; set aside. Gently reheat when needed.

1 Pour off all but 2 tablespoons of the fat from the turkey roasting tin, leaving behind all the dark juices. Put the tin over a medium hob heat, and stir in the flour and honey. Cook, stirring constantly for 1 minute.
2 Gradually mix in the wine, then stock. Cook, stirring constantly until thickened. Bubble for a few minutes. Add any juices from the resting meat. Strain; stir through the mustard (to taste). Serve in a warmed gravy boat.

Turkey Stock for Mustard and Honey Gravy Put the turkey giblets into a large pan. Add 1 sliced onion, 2 chopped carrots, 1 hopped celery stick, 10 peppercorns, 2 bay leaves, 3 thyme sprigs and 1.5 litres (2⅔ pint) cold water. Bring to the boil, then simmer for 1 hour. Strain through a sieve lined with kitchen paper. Cool, then pour into an airtight container and chill for up to 1 day. Makes about 700ml (1¼ pint).

Apple Sauce

The perfect accompaniment for roasted pork or goose.

To serve eight, you will need: 900g (2lb) cooking apples, such as Bramley, peeled, cored and roughly chopped, 50g (2oz) butter, 4 tbsp light muscovado sugar, or to taste.

1 Put the apples into a pan with 4–6 tbsp water. Cover and cook over a low heat for about 10 minutes, stirring occasionally, until the apples are soft and reduced to a pulp.

2 Beat with a wooden spoon until smooth, then rub through a sieve, if you like. Stir in the butter and 2 tbsp of the sugar, then taste and add a little more sugar, if you like. Serve warm or cold.

FREEZE AHEAD

To make ahead and freeze, complete the recipe, then cool and put into a freezerproof container. Label and freeze for up to one month. To use, thaw at cool room temperature. Put into a pan and simmer over a medium heat for 2–3 minutes until heated through.

Cranberry Sauce

A traditional favourite with roast turkey.

To serve eight, you will need:
225g (8oz) fresh cranberries, grated zest and juice of 1 orange, 4 tbsp fine shred marmalade, 125g (4oz) light muscovado sugar, 50ml (2fl oz) port.

1 Put the cranberries into a pan. Add the orange zest and juice, marmalade, sugar and port and mix well.
2 Bring to the boil, then reduce the heat and simmer for 5-10 minutes, stirring occasionally, until thickened.

SAVE TIME

To make ahead and freeze, complete the recipe, then tip into a freezerproof container and cool. Label and freeze for up to one month. To use, thaw and serve warm or cold. To serve warm, put into a pan and simmer over a medium heat for 2-3 minutes until heated through.

Bread Sauce

A traditional sauce to have with roast poultry and game.

To serve eight, you will need:
1 onion, peeled and quartered,
4 cloves, 2 bay leaves, 600ml
(1 pint) milk, 125g (4oz) fresh white
breadcrumbs, 4 tbsp double cream,
25g (1oz) butter, a little freshly grated
nutmeg, salt and freshly ground
black pepper.

1 Stud each onion quarter with a
   clove, then put into a pan with the
   bay leaves and milk. Bring to the
   boil, then take off the heat and
   leave to infuse for 10 minutes.
2 Use a slotted spoon to lift out the
   onion and bay leaves and discard.
   Add the breadcrumbs to the pan
   and bring to the boil, stirring, then
   reduce the heat and simmer for
   5–6 minutes.
3 Stir in the cream and butter, then
   add the nutmeg and season with
   salt and ground black pepper.
   Spoon into a warmed serving dish.

FREEZE AHEAD

To make ahead and freeze,
complete the recipe, then tip into
a freezerproof container and cool.
Label and freeze for up to one month.
To use, thaw at room temperature.
Put into a pan with an extra 2 tbsp
cream and reheat gently, then simmer
for 2 minutes or until piping hot.

Onion Sauce

Serve with roast goose.

To serve eight, you will need:
600ml (1 pint) milk, 2 large onions,
10 peppercorns, 1 large mace blade,
1 large bay leaf, 40g (1½oz) butter,
40g (1½oz) plain flour, freshly grated
nutmeg, salt and freshly ground
black pepper

1 Pour the milk into a pan. Halve
   the onions, cut two thin slices
   off one half and add them to the
   milk; put the rest to one side.
   Add the peppercorns, mace and
   bay leaf and bring almost to the
   boil, then take off the heat, cover
   and leave to infuse for about 20
   minutes. Strain.
2 Meanwhile, finely dice the
   remaining onions and cook in
   15g (½oz) of the butter for 10–15
   minutes until softened.

3 Melt the remaining butter in a
   separate pan, stir in the flour
   and cook, stirring constantly,
   for 1 minute or until cooked but
   not coloured. Take off the heat
   and gradually pour in the milk,
   whisking constantly. Season
   with nutmeg, salt and ground
   black pepper.
4 Add the softened onions, put back
   on to the heat and cook, stirring,
   until the sauce is thickened and
   smooth, then simmer gently for 2
   minutes. Serve warm.

Cumberland Sauce

This sauce is traditionally served cold with hot or cold meats or game.

To serve eight, you will need: finely pared zest and juice of 1 orange, finely pared zest and juice of 1 lemon, 4 tbsp redcurrant jelly, 1 tsp Dijon mustard, 4 tbsp port, pinch of ground ginger (optional), salt and freshly ground black pepper.

1. Cut the citrus zests into fine julienne strips and put into a small pan. Add cold water to cover and simmer for 5 minutes, then drain.
2. Put the orange and lemon juices, citrus zests, redcurrant jelly and mustard into a pan and heat gently, stirring, until the sugar has dissolved. Leave to simmer for 5 minutes, then add the port.
3. Leave to cool. Season with salt and ground black pepper to taste and add a little ginger, if you like.

Mint Sauce

The classic accompaniment for roast lamb. To serve eight, you will need: 1 small bunch of fresh mint, stalks removed, 1–2 tsp golden caster sugar, to taste, 1–2 tbsp wine vinegar, to taste.

1 Finely chop the mint leaves and put into a bowl with the sugar. Stir in 1 tbsp boiling water and put to one side for about 5 minutes to dissolve the sugar.
2 Add the vinegar to taste. Leave to stand for about 1 hour before serving.

Special Mint Jelly

A variation on mint sauce. To serve eight, you will need: grated zest and juice of 1 large orange, 20g (¾oz) freshly chopped mint, 450g (1lb) redcurrant jelly, 4 tbsp balsamic vinegar.

1 Put the orange zest and juice into a pan. Add half the mint and the redcurrant jelly and vinegar. Cook over a low heat for 5 minutes or until smooth. Strain into a serving bowl and stir in the remaining mint.

Cheat's Mint Jelly

This is an ingenious short cut. To serve eight, you will need: 3 sheets leaf gelatine, oil, 200ml (7fl oz) clear apple juice, 1 tbsp white wine vinegar, 1 tsp dried mint.

1 Put the gelatine sheets into a bowl, cover with cold water and leave to soak for 5 minutes.
2 Meanwhile, line a small loaf tin or serving dish with clingfilm, then lightly grease the clingfilm with oil. Pour the apple juice into a small pan, then add the vinegar and mint.
3 Lift out the gelatine (discard the soaking water), add to the pan and heat gently until the gelatine dissolves. Pour the mixture into the prepared tin or dish and leave to cool completely, then chill until set.
4 Invert on to a small board or plate and remove the tin or dish and clingfilm. Cut the jelly into squares and serve.

682 cal ♥ 38g protein
49g fat (21g sat) ♥ 0.9g fibre
17g carb ♥ 1g salt

14

652 cal ♥ 56g protein
38g fat (11g sat) ♥ 1g fibre
22g carb ♥ 2g salt

16

650 cal ♥ 59g protein
37g fat (18g sat) ♥ 2g fibre
39g carb ♥ 1.3g salt

18

With gravy: 286 cal
21g protein ♥ 11g fat (5g sat)
1g fibre ♥ 28g carb ♥ 0.6g salt

20

Calorie Gallery

561 cal ♥ 31g protein
38g fat (9g sat) ♥ 0.1g fibre
20g carb ♥ 0.5g salt

36

585 cal ♥ 68g protein
27g fat (11g sat) ♥ 0g fibre
5g carb ♥ 0.7g salt

38

248 cal ♥ 28g protein
15g fat (4g sat) ♥ 0g fibre
trace carb ♥ 1.3g salt

40

383 cal ♥ 36g protein
23g fat (10g sat) ♥ 1g fibre
23g carb ♥ 1g salt

54

For 8: 729 cal
51g protein ♥ 53g fat (19g sat)
1g fibre ♥ 11g carb ♥ 1.6g salt
For 10: 583 cal ♥ 41g protein
42g fat (15g sat) ♥ 1g fibre
9g carb ♥ 1.3g salt

56

645 cal ♥ 54g protein
51g fat (18g sat) ♥ 0g fibre
0g carb ♥ 0.5g salt

60

230 cal ♥ 13g protein
20g fat (9g sat) ♥ 0g fibre
0.3g carb ♥ 0.3g salt

74

671 cal ♥ 57g protein
47g fat (13g sat) ♥ 1g fibre
11g carb ♥ 2.2g salt

78

601 cals ♥ 60g protein
39g fat (17g sats) ♥ 0.4g
fibre ♥ 2g carb ♥ 0.5g salt

80

645 cal ♥ 54g protein
45g fat (13g sat) ♥ 2g fibre
6g carb ♥ 2g salt

82

301 cal ♥ 21g protein
9g fat (9g sat) ♥ 1g fibre
12g carb ♥ 0.9g salt

161 cal ♥ 4g protein
5g fat (3g sat) ♥ 1g fibre
27g carb ♥ 0.6g salt
26

507 cal ♥ 44g protein
21g fat (8g sat) ♥ 1g fibre
12g carb ♥ 1.2g salt
32

442 cal ♥ 34g protein
27g fat (8g sat) ♥ 2g fibre
13g carb ♥ 1.5g salt
34

830 cal ♥ 44g protein
5g fat (19g sat) ♥ 4g fibre
40g carb ♥ 0.4g salt

769 cal ♥ 52g protein
50g fat (18g sat) ♥ 3g fibre
22g carb ♥ 0.4g salt
48

585 cal ♥ 51g protein
42g fat (15g sat) ♥ 0g fibre
3g carb ♥ 0.3g salt
50

791 cal ♥ 54g protein
55g fat (19g sat) ♥ 2g fibre
15g carb ♥ 0.4g salt
52

574 cal ♥ 49g protein
29g fat (8g sat) ♥ 9g fibre
31g carb ♥ 6g salt

448 cal ♥ 49g protein
26g fat (8g sat) ♥ 0g fibre
5g carb ♥ 6.8g salt
66

583 cal ♥ 34g protein
30g fat (15g sat) ♥ 4g fibre
45g carb ♥ 1.2g salt

467 cal ♥ 36g protein
32g fat (14g sat) ♥ 0.4g salt
6g carb ♥ 0.5g salt
72

70

681 cal ♥ 55g protein
51g fat (18g sat) ♥ 0g fibre
0g carb ♥ 0.4g salt

410 cal ♥ 18g protein
37g fat (14g sat) ♥ 0g fibre
1g carb ♥ 0.2g salt
90

493 cal ♥ 50g protein
28g fat (12g sat) ♥ 0.4g fibre
10g carb ♥ 0.4g salt
92

393 cal ♥ 19g protein
35g fat (12g sat) ♥ 0.3g fibre
1g carb ♥ 0.2g salt
94

Calorie Gallery

488 cal ♥ 25g protein
39g fat (15g sat) ♥ 0.8g fibre
11g carb ♥ 1.2g salt

96

484 cal ♥ 24g protein
42g fat (20g sat) ♥ 0g fibre
1g carb ♥ 0.4g salt

98

510 cal ♥ 58g protein
24g fat (9g sat) ♥ 0g fibre
16g carb ♥ 0.5g salt

102

For 6: 757 cal ♥ 55g prote
62g fat (25g sat) ♥ 0.2g fib
7g carb ♥ 0.7g salt
For 8: 568 cal ♥ 41g prote
47g fat (19g sat) ♥ 0.1g fib
5g carb ♥ 0.5g salt

104

535 cal ♥ 50g protein
29g fat (10g sat) ♥ 0.9g fibre
13g carb ♥ 1.4g salt

120

495 cal ♥ 56g protein
21g fat (5g sat) ♥ 0g fibre
21g carb ♥ 4.8g salt

120

371 cal ♥ 10g protein
28g fat (9g sat) ♥ 3g fibre
20g carb ♥ 0.8g salt

126

165 cal ♥ 2g protein
12g fat (5g sat) ♥ 3g fibre
11g carb ♥ 0.1g salt

136

313 cal ♥ 5g protein
6g fat (5g sat) ♥ 40g fibre
40g carb ♥ 0.2g salt

138

252 cal ♥ 4g protein
18g fat (3g sat) ♥ 5g fibre
19g carb ♥ 0.4g salt

142

36 cal ♥ 0.7g protein
3g fat (0.5g sat) ♥ 0.8g fibre
3g carb ♥ 0g salt
152

46 cal ♥ 0.7g protein
4g fat (2g sat) ♥ 0.1g fibre
3g carb ♥ 0.7g salt
158

122 cal ♥ 0.4g protein
5g fat (3g sat) ♥ 2g fibre
20g carb ♥ trace salt
164

105 cal ♥ 0.2g protein
0g fat ♥ 0.9g fibre
27g carb ♥ trace salt

165

322 cal ♥ 57g protein
8g fat (3g sat) ♥ 0g fibre
4g carb ♥ 0.5g salt

501 cal ♥ 66g protein
26g fat (10g sat) ♥ 0.6g fibre
1.5g carb ♥ 0.4g salt

499 cal ♥ 38g protein
27g fat (14g sat) ♥ 3g fibre
14g carb ♥ 0.2g salt

802 cal ♥ 58g protein
53g fat (15g sat) ♥ 0.8g fibre
27g carb ♥ 2.4g salt

108

114

116

454 cal ♥ 12g protein
22g fat (10g sat) ♥ 9g fibre
49g carb ♥ 0.8g salt

189 cal ♥ 5g protein
14g fat (6g sat) ♥ 2g fibre
11g carb ♥ 0.9g salt

438 cal ♥ 15g protein
24g fat (9g sat) ♥ 5g fibre
38g carb ♥ 0.7g salt

192 cal ♥ 2g protein
19g fat (8g sat) ♥ 4g fibre
4g carb ♥ 0.2g salt

130

132

134

251 cal ♥ 5g protein
8g fat (3g sat) ♥ 7g fibre
43g carb ♥ 1.9g salt

198 cal ♥ 3g protein
8g fat (3g sat) ♥ 2g fibre
30g carb ♥ 0.1g salt

74 cal ♥ 1g protein
5g fat (2g sat) ♥ 2g fibre
6g carb ♥ 0.1g salt

251 cal ♥ 4g protein
10g fat (1g sat) ♥ 9g fibre
39g carb ♥ 0.2g salt

146

148

150

165 cal ♥ 4g protein
0g fat (6g sat) ♥ 0.3g fibre
16g carb ♥ 0.4g salt

113 cal ♥ 3g protein
7g fat (5g sat) ♥ 0.5g fibre
9g carb ♥ 0.1g salt

39 cal ♥ 0.1g protein
0g fat ♥ 0g fibre
8g carb ♥ 0.1g salt

4 cal ♥ 0g protein
0g fat ♥ 0g fibre
1g carb ♥ 0g salt

167

168

169

Index

PICTURE CREDITS

Photographers:
Nicki Dowey (pages 31, 41, 79,
97, 117, 119 and 168T); Gareth
Morgans (pages 19, 21, 23, 25,
57, 59, 105 and 107); Myles New
(pages 17, 71, 75, 93 and 99); Craig
Robertson (pages 9, 10, 11, 14, 15,
33, 35, 37, 39, 45, 46, 49, 51, 53, 62,
63, 65, 67, 77, 81, 83, 84, 85, 87, 88,
89, 95, 103, 109, 110, 111, 112, 115,
121, 123, 127, 129, 133, 135, 137, 139,
143, 145, 151, 154, 156, 157, 159,
164, 165, 166 and 167); Lucinda
Symons (pages 91, 131 and 168B);
Kate Whitaker (pages 55, 61, 73,
147, 149 and 153); Rachel Whiting
(front cover).

Home Economists:
Joanna Farrow, Emma Jane
Frost, Teresa Goldfinch,
Alice Hart, Lucy McKelvie,
Kim Morphew, Aya Nishimura,
Bridget Sargeson,
Stella Sargeson Kate Trend and
Mari Mererid Williams.

Stylists:
Tamzin Ferdinando, Wei Tang,
Helen Trent and Fanny Ward.

BAKE ME A CAKE

There's always time for cake

EASY PEASY MEALS

Easy meals for every day

LET'S DO BRUNCH

Mouth-watering meals to start your day

CHEAP EATS

Budget-busting ideas that won't break the bank

SALAD DAYS

Oh-so-fresh ideas for fabulous salads

Available online

and

from all good bookshops

POSH NOSH

Delicious recipes to impress your guests

PARTY FOOD

Delicious recipes to get the party started

SLOW STOPPERS

Slow-cooked meals packed with flavour

GREAT VEG

Inspired ideas for delicious veggie meals

AL FRESCO EATS

Easy grills, barbecues and picnics

ROAST IT

There's nothing better than a delicious roast

FLASH IN THE PAN

Spice up your noodles and stir-fries

GLUTEN-FREE AND EASY

Oh-so-good-for-you recipes that taste great

LOW FAT LOW CAL

Nice recipes don't need to be naughty